MW00366605

Cook Your Date Into Bed

To my cats,
Chas Michael Michaels and Delia Smith,
for making every other line of this manuscript read
'p-047;;;;;pvsffnnnfei@@".'L[3'

Cook Your Date Into Bed

A collection of recipes and stories from the
complex world of courtship

Helen Graves

DOG 'n' BONE

Published in 2014 by Dog 'n' Bone Books
An imprint of Ryland Peters & Small Ltd

20–21 Jockey's Fields   519 Broadway, 5th Floor
London WC1R 4BW   New York, NY 10012

www.rylandpeters.com

10 9 8 7 6 5 4 3 2 1

Text © Helen Graves 2014
Design and illustration © Dog 'n' Bone Books 2014

A CIP catalog record for this book is available from
the Library of Congress and the British Library.

ISBN: 978 1 909313 14 9

Printed in China

Editors: Clare Sayer and Pete Jorgensen
Designer: Jerry Goldie
Illustration: Kate Sutton

For digital editions, visit www.cicobooks.com/apps.php

Acknowledgments:

Thank you to Mum and Dad for getting over the fact that "it's their little
girl writing slightly naughty things." Thank you to Pete and Mark at
Dog 'n' Bone for being patient and letting me do what I want. Thank you
to Scott 'Big Face' Williams for the picnic song suggestion and to Florian
Siepert for re-introducing me to the wonder of R Kelly's 'Ignition'. Thank
you to Sally Butcher for the dates fried in butter idea, to Kerstin Rodgers
for her Mustardy Mary recipe, to Marcus Bawdon for teaching me about
'dirty veg', to John Gionleka for teaching me how to cook lobster, and to
Felix Cohen for his hot buttered rum recipe.

Thank you to Donald for helping me to create Peckham Korean Fried
Chicken, for keeping me sane, and for eating and getting drunk with me.

And a huge thank you to all my mates and Twitter followers who let me
publish their dating stories. This book would have been a lot less funny
without the tales of your misfortunes.

Contents

Introduction   6

Chapter One   **The Dinner Date**   12

Chapter Two   **The Morning After**   40

Chapter Three   **The Drunk Date**   52

Chapter Four   **The Movie Date**   60

Chapter Five   **The Picnic Date**   66

Chapter Six   **The BBQ Date**   76

Chapter Seven   **Aphrodisiacs**   90

Chapter Eight   **Balls Out Banger**   102

Chapter Nine   **When Good Dates Go Bad**   116

Index   128

Introduction

The Ground Rules

Crikey, this is hard. It's hard because, well, who has ever written anything about cooking for your "date" that wasn't a terrible cheesy pile of utter crap? To be honest, I don't know why I took this job on. Bloody hell. Can I quit now? No? Shit. I mean, sugar. Oh hell, look, there might be some swearing. There will be some swearing. OK, fine, let's get some ground rules established now:

1 There will be swearing.

2 There will be lists. Numbered lists. I like lists and I like to number them.

3 There will be much talk of **BOOZE**. I make no apologies for this.

4 I hate the word "date." It's so… cringey and old-fashioned in a bad way and… look, we're not in *Grease*. (Who did you want to be? I wanted to be Rizzo until I grew up and realized that, actually, she was a bit, erm, "loose.") The thing is, the sales team liked the title, so what could I do? (Think of a better title, apparently. I couldn't think of a better title.)

5 Cooking in order to impress another person is a beautiful gesture, it really is, but we definitely need to establish some boundaries. Here goes:
TRADITIONAL "DATE FOOD" IS LAME. A typical menu from a mainstream food website would likely include seared scallops for a starter, a fillet steak for a main, and then some kind of chocolate-based dessert. Now there's nothing wrong with any of those ingredients per se, it's just that, like the concept of cooking for a date, they are, well, for want of a better word, somewhat dated. What happened to having fun? Why do we have to have silly rules? Why the lack of imagination? The truth of the matter is that "romantic" or "sexy" food (yep, really hard not to make it sound lame) is anything that is cooked well, with thought and a little imagination; anything that is cooked with care and attention—although, saying that, we cannot dismiss the importance of…

CONTEXT. The traditional dinner date is fine and all, but who does that nowadays? I know you're all modern as hell so let's think about it. The modern date isn't even defined as such, thank goodness. It is possible to actually just go out and have fun with another person, without defining the situation! Who knew? That is why I have organized this book into "potential scenarios." Let us break away from the shackles of convention. Hell, if we're going to talk about going on a "date," then we may as well talk about getting to "third base." A bowl of instant noodles, pimped with emergency supplies bought from the convenience store or corner

shop on the way home from the pub, bar, or club can be just as seductive and I will tell you why right now. The reason is that the most seductive of all ingredients is...

FUN. Having a laugh. Making someone else smile. That's what it's all about after all, isn't it?

Crikey, I almost sound serious.

Consider this book a guide to how to cook your date into bed, while also being anti-dating. Make sense? No, OK. How about this: consider it a way to construct a plate of food that will get you laid. Hahaha. Sorry. OK, serious face. Consider it a cynical look at the world of food and courtship and how they fit together; a myth-decimating bomb on the ass of every single "meal for two," "Valentines menu," and "steak for him, salad for her" lazy, trite, and downright patronizing menu ever written. There will be cocktails, there will be recipes, and there will be a lot of cliché-busting ranting.

Now don't go giving me that disappointed face. I mean it. I'm not dodging the task at hand, really I'm not. I'm just saying that cooking for someone you want to see more of doesn't have to be about schmoozing or ticking boxes or pretending you're something you're not. It's about freakin' **SURVIVAL**, goddammit! It's about dealing with any situation, positive or negative. At the age of 33, I have learned that most situations can be handled with food or booze, and dating is no different.

Let us begin.

CHAPTER ONE

The Dinner Date

Cooking For Your Date

This chapter filled me with fear, but the classic dinner date scenario has to be covered, so here we are. Why the apprehension? I dunno, maybe I just like to imagine myself bucking the trend and doing terribly modern things like going on "breakfast dates" to Balthazar, as I imagine people do in New York. Maybe they do. I live in London, however, and I can bet you won't catch many Londoners doing breakfast dates. The idea has just made me laugh out loud, actually; Londoners can barely stomach the fact that other people are **DARING TO EXIST** as we move about the city in the morning, and we certainly do not want to sit around relishing the company of another **AIR THIEF**, voluntarily, on a **WEEKDAY**. I'm barely functional before 11 a.m., and anyway, trying to impress someone with wit, intelligence, and attractiveness first thing in the morning is just making life a whole lot harder than it needs to be. No. The real reason I think there's a problem surfacing here is that the evening dinner scenario is where there is the most potential for fist-in-mouth, knuckle-biting clichés. What happened? When did "date food" become so tarnished with corny associations?

I blame the eighties. No, really. I was an eighties child, and formative years were spent watching soap operas and movies; fictional dates played out in front of susceptible eyes. Think about it. Everything that's cheesy about the image of a candlelit dinner has something very eighties about it. The very mention of the words "dinner date" brings to mind boxes of Black Magic chocolates, black satin... I don't know why black satin but still, it's there. Barry White is playing in the background, Babycham pops open, the black forest gateau is chilling in the fridge, and you're hoping for some action on the water bed later. Everything about it just seems, well, a bit tense, actually, which brings me nicely to my first bit of advice about cooking dinner for your date.

It is incredibly important to **STAY RELAXED**. Cooking a meal for another person is a truly lovely gesture, and an experience that should be enjoyed, not feared. The way to do this is to keep things simple. Now it might be the case that you're a highly talented chef who can't wait to show off your shit-hot mad skillz, in which case, what the hell are you doing reading this book, doofus?! Just get in the

kitchen already. You need to get the sous vide up to temperature! If, however, you're "normal," then let me show the way... **THE WAY OF STEAK**. A perfectly cooked steak is hard to beat, really (provided your date eats meat, of course... don't fall at the final hurdle). There is, however, a right way to do it versus lots of wrong ways. If you follow exactly the method outlined on the following pages, then you will have possibly the best steak of your—and, crucially, your date's—life. Promise.

Menu

MAIN COURSE:

Rib-eye steak
Herb salad with
cherry tomato vinaigrette

DESSERT:

The most glorious of Knickerbockers

TO DRINK:

The perfect martini

The Ultimate Steak Dinner

The success of this lies not only in the cooking method but also in the quality of the meat. You can buy cheap meat, sure, and you can cook it as I have specified below, but you will still end up with a cheap piece of meat; there isn't going to be any major transformation. This is a recipe, not a magic spell. Buy the best meat you can afford—this is the time to splash out—and always buy meat from a proper butcher. I would recommend rib-eye, because it has a decent amount of fat and therefore flavor. Fillet is fine, but it's prized for its soft texture, not beefy flavor. Rib-eye every time. Repeat: rib-eye every time.

A Perfect Steak

This recipe uses one large steak, because it is much easier to cook a large steak well than it is two smaller ones. Slice thickly before serving on separate plates, or on one plate to share, depending on how relaxed you are about these things. Personally, I hate sharing food—it winds me up, I like to know what's mine—but hey, do what you like (just not with the cooking).

Ingredients

1 rib-eye steak, approximately
16–20 oz (450–550 g)

Salt and freshly ground
black pepper

Heavy-based cast-iron griddle pan to
cook the steak (or use a barbecue)

Serves 2

1 Take your steak out of the fridge at least an hour before you
want to cook it, to bring it up to room temperature. Next, open
the windows: this cooking method is going to create some smoke,
and it's going to set the smoke alarm off if you don't let it out.

2 Place the griddle pan over a high heat and heat until it is so
hot that you can't hold your hand over it. Do not add any oil
to the pan—the high heat will stop the steak from sticking.

3 Season the steak on both sides and very generously indeed.
Add more salt and pepper than you think is sensible. Trust
me. Add the steak to the pan.

4 You will need to turn the steak regularly, say every minute.
This is the best way to ensure a well-cooked steak with a
great crust outside and juicy meat within. Two to three minutes
each side should do it, and remember: turn frequently. It is not
advisable to cook a rib-eye rare, because it doesn't allow any of
the glorious fat inside to melt. Medium-rare should be fine. If
you like your steak very rare, choose a different cut.

5 When the steak is done, put it on a warm plate to rest for
5–10 minutes. This is ESSENTIAL. Slice and serve.

Ooh, Saucy

There are a number of options when it comes to a sauce for your steak. Some people don't like any sauce, which is fine. Some like to have mustard (I have been known to have three types of mustard with my steak—now that's living), while others like a flavored butter, kicked up with herbs, chili, or (my favorite) anchovy. Problem is, that little disc of often-too-cold butter just looks a bit crap. A bit 1992. There are of course the more interesting contenders, such as Italian salsa verde (a mixture of capers, anchovies, mustard, and herbs), old-school sauces, such as peppercorn (a bit too "steakhouse" for me), chimichurri, or the sinful king of steak sauces: béarnaise. I've given recipes for the last two. Nice to have options, innit?

Béarnaise

Béarnaise sauce isn't particularly difficult to make, it just requires a bit of elbow grease. So eat your spinach. It also works wonders with rib-eye steaks.

Ingredients

4 tsp tarragon vinegar

3 free-range egg yolks

8 oz (225 g) butter, melted

2 tbsp tarragon leaves, chopped

Salt

Serves 2

1 Place a glass bowl over a pan of barely simmering water, making sure the bottom of the bowl doesn't touch the water. Put the egg yolks and vinegar into the bowl and whisk over the heat for 10 minutes, until the mixture thickens.

2 Slowly add the melted butter, whisking gently until thick again. Add the tarragon leaves and season with salt. Turn off the heat and leave the bowl over the water until ready to serve.

Chimichurri

This punchy Argentinian sauce is a potent mix of herbs and chili that's fabulous with barbecued steaks (and, FYI, fish). It does contain raw garlic, however, so I leave it up to you to choose between impressing your date with a stonking sauce, or keeping your breath garlic-free. If you choose the latter, just make this sauce for your friends instead. Or just yourself. Just make the sauce at some point, basically.

Ingredients

4 cloves of garlic

Large handful of flat-leaf parsley leaves

Sprig of fresh oregano, leaves picked

1 shallot

2 tsp hot chili flakes (or to taste)

2 tbsp red wine vinegar

1 tbsp lime juice

Olive oil

Salt

Serves 2

1. Either chop the garlic, parsley, oregano, and shallot very finely or whizz in a food processor. Mix in the chili flakes, vinegar, and lime juice.

2. Add enough olive oil to loosen to a sauce-like consistency. Season with salt.

Herb Salad with Cherry Tomato Vinaigrette

It is frankly rather baffling to me that steaks often come with very heavy side dishes. Mac and cheese, fries, mashed potato—all lovely things, but a really decent hunk of steak is incredibly filling and you are trying to impress another person with your culinary prowess here, not send them to sleep nursing a food baby. This salad is the answer to that potential problem.

Ingredients

3 tbsp extra-virgin olive oil

2 handfuls cherry tomatoes (different colors if possible), halved

1 tbsp red wine vinegar

Salt and freshly ground black pepper

1 bag prepared herb salad or a mixture of salad leaves and herbs such as chives, tarragon, parsley, chervil

Serves 2

1 Heat 1 tablespoon of the olive oil in a pan and gently cook the tomatoes until they begin to soften, around 5 minutes. Roughly squish a few of the tomatoes in the pan.

2 Add the vinegar, remaining olive oil, and salt and pepper. Mix together and then use to dress the herb salad.

To Drink:

The Perfect Martini

You're going to need a drink that makes you look impressive and classy. This means that you need a martini. There is never a bad time to drink a martini; at least, I haven't discovered it yet. It's the perfect drink—strong, pure, delicious, and it hits the spot with alarming precision. Just be careful. To quote James Thurber, "One martini is all right. Two are too many, and three are not enough."

Like cooking steak, there is a right way to make a martini, and I will have no arguments on this matter. Firstly, a martini is made with gin. It is not made with vodka. Not in my house. If you want vodka, make a different drink. My preferred gin brand is Beefeater. It's a good, solid gin that has crisp aromatics with none of that overly floral crap. Secondly, you need to chill your martini glass, so pop it in the freezer at least an hour before. If you don't chill the glass then you don't make a martini. Back off. This recipe will make a stonking martini. Do not deviate from it.

Ingredients

1 very well-chilled martini glass

3 fl oz (90 ml) gin

1 capful Noilly Pratt dry vermouth, cold

Crushed ice

1 twist (cut a strip of lemon peel, making sure you remove any white pith)

Serves 1

1. Combine the gin and vermouth in a cocktail shaker. Add a good handful of ice and stir for 2 minutes. Don't shake it because you'll end up with loads of little shards of ice, which will water down your martini.

2. When condensation appears on the outside of the cocktail shaker, strain and pour into a very well-chilled martini glass. Hold the lemon peel over the top of the glass and fold it in half until you see a little spray. That's as much lemon as you need. Serve at once.

Dessert

The way you go with dessert depends on your date's preferences (read: stamina). You've just eaten a steak. Many people would therefore choose something light to follow, and I wonder if this is because they don't know about ice cream? Must be. The wonderful thing about ice cream—apart from the obvious outrageous deliciousness—is that you can buy some really good-quality stuff in the shops and just do a little bit of fluffing and jazzing at the last minute. In doing so you strike the perfect balance between having put in a little bit of thought and effort, and looking too effortlessly cool to go stressing yourself by going beyond the call of duty. If you're really not up for the ice cream, however, there's another path for you my friend, and that is number 6 on this list.

Here are some ways to preen, fluff, flatter, and pimp up your store-bought ice cream, to marvelous effect.

1 Soak some raisins in Pedro Ximenez sherry and serve over vanilla ice cream. Pour a little extra sherry over the ice cream and serve. That's sexy. Truly.

2 Crystallized rose petals, herbs, or other edible flowers make a beautiful and subtly flavored topping for a relatively plain ice cream such as vanilla. A real "ta-da!" of a topping, to be honest. Make sure the petals (or leaves) are not sprayed. For rose petals, first snip off the white heel, as this part is quite bitter. Hold the base of each petal and brush lightly with beaten egg white, then sprinkle evenly with superfine

(caster) sugar and lay out on a baking sheet lined with non-stick baking paper to dry for a few hours. Edible flowers include rose petals, pansies, violets, primroses, and lavender. Good examples of herbs that would be up to the task include thyme and mint.

3 Sprinkle raspberries with rosewater and use as a topping. Very fragrant.

4 This is an idea I have flagrantly nicked from my mate Sally, who runs an Iranian shop and deli called Persepolis in Peckham, south London, where I live. She has plenty of Persian flavor tricks up her sleeve and this is possibly one of the greatest ice cream toppings of all time. Fry a couple of handfuls of mixed nuts and some roughly chopped dates in butter. Serve on top of the ice cream.

5 The Most Glorious of Knickerbockers. Knickerbocker glory? What? Now don't be a snob. Try the recipe on page 26.

6 Stop being a wimp.

The Most Glorious of Knickerbockers

I understand an ice cream sundae may sound a little bit TGI Friday's, but actually, when made well, this is a fun dessert. Just make sure you get the right glassware—you know the one—tall, silly, over the top. There's also potential for the dreaded sharing, if that so floats your boat.

Ingredients

Salted caramel ice cream

Popcorn (caramel works well)

Vanilla ice cream

Chocolate sauce (you can buy this ready prepared but make sure to choose a good-quality sauce)

A handful of pecan nuts, roughly chopped

1 Start with a scoop of salted caramel ice cream, followed by some popcorn, then vanilla ice cream then some popcorn and so on.

2 Add a final layer of popcorn, then pour over some chocolate sauce. Garnish with chopped pecan nuts. Phwoar.

chopped nuts

chocolate sauce

vanilla ice cream

popcorn

caramel ice cream

Cooking With Your Date: The Cook Off

There is of course the possibility of getting your date involved with the cooking, and here I advise you to tread carefully. Your date may not be that into cooking, and if they see it as a chore, then they're just going to think you're a lazy-ass loser who is trying to share the load. If, on the other hand, they are Into Food Big Time, then you're onto a winner. Cooking with another person can be really fun, and it provides a focus to ease jangling nerves. Also, if it goes wrong, not only can you have a laugh about it, but you are BOTH TO BLAME. Genius. This leads me rather nicely to what I think is my favorite dating story of all time, courtesy of my mate Cynthia (a fake name which I let her choose). Just to give you a bit of context... I write about food, as you've probably noticed, which means that I have a lot of friends who are also very much into food. In fact, I think all my friends are. Anyway, Cynthia is one such friend and this is her story of what was basically, for her, the perfect date. I have provided some footnotes because, quite frankly, I do not expect everyone else to be such massive food nerds as we are. Here is the story directly from the woman herself:

Cynthia's Story: A Food Geek Off

So... we met through an online dating website. I think it was the mention of his undying love for brawn and St. John donuts* that prompted an approach from me.

Anyway, we have all the banter, mainly food-related, and I throw in a challenge—a cook off! So we arrange our first date: each buys ingredients for the other person, we swap, we have 3 hours to cook, then we serve a mash-up tasting menu. (We've actually already had a first date, to make sure the other isn't a psycho.)

I arrive, and he's laid out a board of Calabrian cheese and 'nduja** (THREE YEARS AGO, BEFORE IT WAS ON-TREND. KNOB.) We drink white tea he brought back from Japan. I am obviously toe-curlingly in love already. We both prepare to exchange mystery ingredients. He presents me with a St. John tote filled with confit duck leg, French blueberries, smoked GP*** streaky bacon, Puy lentils, Jersey Royal potatoes, parsley, cream, and some Calabrian chilies (he knows they're my favorite ingredient, but he also knows I cannot shoe-horn them into this meal). And then I find, nestled at the bottom, a whole fucking truffle. !?!?!?!?

I give him… a pig's head—though mercifully separated into ears, brain, cheeks, and tongue—four trotters, tail, ribs, tamarind, mint, carrots, lemongrass, chilies, garlic, shallots, fish sauce, Sriracha****.

We ended up with a sketchbook full of the food we cooked and ate together… and later he…

— The Menu —

Him: Crispy brain, tongue, tail, and ear, with parsley and wholegrain mustard.

Me: Potted duck with morel mushrooms, duck scratchings, and a blueberry compote.

Him: Vietnamese soup made with a trotter stock, coconut-braised pig's cheek, and slow-cooked tamarind and honey spare ribs.

Me: Truffled potato dauphinoise and Puy lentils braised with bacon, topped with crispy bacon rinds. (Note the crispy animal fat theme with my menu.)

Him: Mint sorbet.

Me: Blueberry ripple ice cream.

OK, so the end of the story is so heartbreaking I can't even begin to tell you what she wrote. Sorry. Basically they are no longer together and we now refer to him by a name that is… well, it's not his real name, put it that way.

Seriously though, what a date! If you, however, make up part of the other 99.9% of the population that isn't as geeky about food as we are, and you don't want to feel like you're in the semi-finals of *MasterChef*, but you would still like to have a bash at cooking with your date, then the recipe that follows is a good place to start.

* St. John is a restaurant in London, famous for serving offal and the gnarliest bits of animals, plus outrageously good custard-filled donuts.
** 'Nduja is a spicy, spreadable sausage from Calabria which is now very trendy.
*** GP stands for Ginger Pig, which is a very famous British butcher and purveyor of high-quality meat.
**** Sriracha is a type of hot sauce.

My Drunk Kitchen

I didn't think it fair to include my mates' dating stories without including one of my own, so here it is. This is reproduced from my blog, Food Stories. I wrote this in May 2012. We're still together. Drunken cooking works. I refer to him in the text as "my friend," probably because I didn't want to freak him out at the time, even though we were sleeping together. Weird. Anyway.

Helen's Story: Paralytic Poultry In Peckham

This is a recipe that was concocted by me and my friend when we were drunk; I'm not going to lie. It started thus:

"Let's make Korean fried chicken!"

"OK!"

"But let's make it like, you know, better and shit! We'll stamp the style of Peckham all over those birds and then deep-fry them! TWICE!"

"OK!" (sound of drool hitting the floor)

Because deep-frying when drunk is always a smart idea...

Peckham Korean Fried Chicken™

So, we went out immediately and bought some chicken wings, which now reveals that we were in fact drunk in the middle of the day. We had no recipe to hand, so we started poking about on the Internet, as you do. After a while, the maelstrom of different methods, ingredients, and opinions made our heads spin and we began to approach things according to the rules of drunken logic; that is to say, we decided to wing it by borrowing random ideas and ingredients willy-nilly to create one unholy mother of a mash-up. I expect I've totally sold this recipe to you by now, so without further ado, here's how to make your very own drunken batch of pure PKFC™.

To make the marinade for the wings

Ingredients

10 chicken wings

2 cloves garlic

1 tbsp gojujang
(Korean chili paste),
rechristened as
Kajagoogoo

Milk

Serves 2

1 Begin by putting some Wu Tang on the stereo. Turn it up loud, the bass will help with step 3.

2 Now you can marinate your chicken wings. Start by vigorously pounding two cloves of garlic in a pestle and mortar. Stick this in a bowl and add one generous tablespoon of gojujang (Korean chili paste). Immediately rename said chili paste "Kajagoogoo" upon discovery that you cannot remember how to pronounce gojujang properly because it is an unfamiliar word and you are hosed.

3 Complete the marinade by adding enough milk to comfortably submerge the chicken in a spicy bath. Plunge your hands into the bowl and start rubbing and fondling the wings, while saying things like "horny," "hubba," and "massage my meat." Film your friend doing this on your iPhone. Both regularly fold in on yourselves in fits of giggles. Put the wings to one side.

To fry, fry…
hush, hush,
Peckham Rye

Ingredients

1½ cups (150 g) all-purpose (plain) flour

1¼ cups (200 g) cornstarch (cornflour)

1½ tsp baking powder

1 tbsp sesame seeds

2 dried red chilis

1 star anise

1 tsp ground ginger

Old Bay Seasoning (optional)

¼ tsp MSG (most definitely optional)

1 can of Red Stripe, or any other lager you can find

Salt and pepper, to taste

To make the batter for the wings

1 Put some K-pop on. Turn it up loud.

2 Next, harrumph the flour, cornstarch (cornflour), baking powder, and a pinch of salt into a bowl and set about making it sexy. You're aiming to create a flavor bomb and drop it on batter city, yo. Boom!

3 Start by toasting the sesame seeds, then pounding, pounding, pounding them (vigorously) in a pestle and mortar along with the dried chilis, star anise, ground ginger, and, er, a touch of Old Bay Seasoning because you're drunk and at the time you're thinking it's a great idea. Next, rain down a little chemical magic on that party by adding the MSG, just for shits and giggles.

4 Mix the batter with half the can of Red Stripe beer you're holding at the time plus an equal quantity of water; aim for a thick slurry that gloops off the tip of each chicken wing in explicit, quivering ribbons. This should be outrageously funny, so if it isn't, that means the texture is wrong. Add more flour or beer until you reach the uncontrollable, shoulder-shaking stage of laughter.

Ingredients

2 cloves garlic

1 onion, grated

Thumb-sized piece of ginger, grated

2 tbsp vegetable oil, for frying

1 tbsp pounded rock sugar

4 tbsp Kajagoogoo, plus extra

Groundnut (peanut) or vegetable oil for deep-frying, enough to comfortably submerge the wings

Chopped scallions (spring onions) and sesame seeds, to garnish

To make the sauce

1 Put *Milkshake* by Kelis on. Turn it up loud.

2 Heat up the vegetable oil in a pan. Crush the garlic cloves and cook it in the pan with the grated onion, ginger, (vigorously) pounded rock sugar, and Kajagoogoo. Set aside.

3 Heat your oil for deep-frying. This should be done with the utmost care and attention, ideally while not drunk and not holding a can of beer. One should definitely not walk away from the pan, leaving it unattended. In fact, just don't ever do this unless you're a complete and utter tool.

4 Use a small piece of crumpet to test if the oil is hot enough (because you don't have any bread). If the temperature is correct, the crumpet should take about 60 seconds to brown. When hot, slip each wing into the batter and pull it out slowly so that it looks kind of rude; give props to the comedy noises and visuals. Lower into the hot oil 2 wings at a time, and let them fry for about 4 minutes (total stab in the dark on the timings). Drain on paper towel. When all are done, fry them all a second time until golden all over. Drain again.

5 Slap the wings about in the Kajagoogoo sauce a bit until they're more or less covered. Pile onto a plate and garnish with chopped scallions (spring onions) and sesame seeds. Serve with a roll of paper towel, a massively smug expression, and an outfit that EXACTLY matches the color of the Kajagoogoo. You'll see. Revel in the funky fermented chili heat and sticky sweetness, the filthy satisfaction at having double-deep-fried some meat (vigorously). PKFC™ sounds like a chemical abbreviation and it may as well be, considering all the stuff that went into this recipe. I haven't mentioned thus far the teaspoon of raspberry jam we added "for a laugh"— now that's living.

If you have any leftover chicken it is possible to make the hangover breakfast of joy, which consists of clumsily picked leftover wing meat and the odd piece of batter fried with onion and topped with an egg.

In conclusion

You know what? These could actually be great, pending a few improvements…

Improvements needed

1 Swap the half water/half beer mix for all beer to make the batter lighter. It was kinda thick and spongy. Also, increase the quantity of liquid (same reason).

2 Use less Kajagoogoo in the sauce; that shit is intense and the overall effect was cloying.

3 The raspberry jam probably isn't necessary…

4 Buy an oil thermometer to reduce anxiety.

5 Be more responsible.

6 Make more fried chicken in general.

7 Do more exercise.

8 Make more of an effort with the recycling.

9 Stop swearing so much.

10 Get your roots done.

To Drink:

Wrongungina

This is a drunk kitchen, so you are going to need a drink. Sophistication is not really the name of the game in the drunk kitchen, so I would suggest something a little bit silly instead. I present to you the Wrongungina. This drink is so called because it is a mixture of Orangina and raki, a Turkish anise-flavored drink. It's pretty pokey, pretty full on, very tasty, and just a little bit wrong. That is why we like it. The drink is served at my boyfriend's restaurant, Peckham Bazaar, and is actually rather popular.

Ingredients

Ice

1 fl oz (25 ml) raki

1 bottle Orangina

Add some ice to a glass. Pour the raki in and top up with the Orangina. Serve with a cheeky grin.

CHAPTER two

The Morning After

Breakfast Highs

I want to kick things off on a positive note by inviting you to imagine that the date has gone well. Really well. So well, in fact, that your date is still present in the morning. Hopefully they're somewhere in your vicinity and not, say, passed out face down on the living-room floor. Imagine they're snoozing gently beside you, their face a vision of peaceful slumber as they dream of kittens, ice cream, and cotton candy.

Now I don't want to be presumptuous, but I'm going to wager that there was a high chance that alcohol was involved last night. When your date awakes, that bubble of fluffy happy dreamy joy is going to burst like an angry spleen and empty its furious, acidic, hungover juices onto your parade. What you need to do is head it off with…

Eggs.

You heard.

A Good Egg

Now there are two ways of approaching an early morning egg cooking situation (well, three actually, but I'll get to that shortly), and they all depend on how you feel about eggs. I'm going to start by giving you two recipes: one for the most dreamy, perfect scrambled eggs in the entire world, and one (dons cap of sophistication) for Eggy Crumpets.

Now, eggy crumpets are ace. They are what one would describe as a bit filthy, meaning they slot right into the hangover repertoire, stand to attention, and salute. Perfect scrambled eggs, on the other hand, should not be made by anyone who doesn't fully appreciate the splendor of this quintessential breakfast ingredient. If you are the kind of person who cooks your scrambled eggs to oblivion, until they are a bitty, rubbery mess, then you can step the hell away from my recipe, quite frankly. You don't deserve it. If you want to experience scrambled eggs of pure silken pleasure, the actual Best Scrambled Eggs Of All Time, however, then this, THIS, is the recipe for you.

Donald's Perfect Scrambled Eggs

You may like to get busy with the garnish—smoked salmon, chives, chorizo, yada yada yada. That's all fine. I mean, it's your life after all. Personally, I like to keep scrambled eggs simple, and so what I'm going to teach you here is all method. It's really easy, really fast, and just incredibly impressive. The reason that most people fluff scrambled eggs is because they are SCARED. Scared of the eggs not being cooked. This is their downfall, the barrier that lies between them and eggy perfection. This is actually my boyfriend's recipe, and the first time he cooked it for me, man, was I impressed. Now I'm just like, "Er, I **said** I wanted **boiled**," but back then I was swooning all over the shop.

Ingredients

2 eggs

½ stick (50 g) lightly salted butter

2 slices toast

Slightly more salt than you think you need

Freshly ground pepper (black of course is great, but I'm a big fan of white pepper with eggs)

Serves 1

1 Crack the eggs into a small bowl and season with the salt and pepper. Lob the butter into a small pan on a low heat. When the butter is starting to melt, pour in the eggs and give them a gentle stir. The trick is to keep stirring them gently over this low heat, so they don't stick to the bottom of the pan. DO NOT under any circumstances start mixing them furiously, or "beating" them; this is where people go wrong, which is understandable, given the use of the word "scrambled." Don't actively scramble, just tease the eggs around the pan.

2 When they look like they are almost cooked—I said ALMOST—remove from the heat and pour onto toast. The residual heat will continue cooking the eggs, and by the time they get to your gob, they'll be perfect.

Eggy Crumps

There is actually nothing sophisticated about this, but it will hit the spot, I promise you. It's like super-charged eggy bread. Think about it—the crumpet is full of holes, holes that are made to be filled with egg and fried in butter.

Ingredients

2 eggs

Splash of milk

½ stick (50 g) butter

2 crumpets

Salt and freshly ground black pepper

Serves 2

1 Beat the eggs lightly in a small bowl, add a splash of milk, and season with salt and pepper.

2 Melt the butter in a frying pan and while this is happening, dip the crumpets into the egg mixture, turning them over a few times so they absorb the egg.

3 Fry each crumpet in the butter until golden on both sides. Eat with brown sauce or tomato ketchup, if you like. A bit of hot sauce never did anyone any harm.

Mumbai Disco Fry Eggs

But hang on, I hear you saying, I'm not some smooth-ass scrambler, and I ain't no filthbag eggy crump-monger neither—I'm a spicy renegade, goddammit! No problem. You're a free spirit, I get it. You cannot be bound by the rules of scrambling, or crumping. Rules schmules.

For you, then, you real fly guy/sister, I present MUMBAI DISCO FRY EGGS. OK, now stay with me. I first made this recipe because I found a video on YouTube—a video of a guy making this on a street stall in India. It looked so brilliant that I made it sharpish and so help me if it didn't turn out to be the best hangover cure of all time. Apparently the recipe is actually called... no, I'm not telling you; the truth is just so mundane, so awful in its unremarkableness that I refuse to taint your enjoyment by letting it slip. This is a recipe for the kitchen adventurer, and I leave it to you to test the mettle of your date. One thing you don't need to worry about is the mixture in the pan looking a mess. It will taste brilliant, I promise. Anyway, the messy edges give you the crispy bits of joy that you so desire.

Ingredients

Oil, for frying

3 green chilies, sliced (or more or less to taste)

2 eggs

Pinch each of chili powder, turmeric, and garam masala

Salt

2 small soft round rolls, 1 large soft round roll, or 1 hot dog bun, split

Handful of fresh cilantro (coriander)

Handful of finely sliced scallions (spring onions)

Serves 2

1 Heat a frying pan or skillet over a medium-high heat and add some oil (a couple of tablespoons should do it). When hot, add half the chilies and fry briefly. Add the eggs and break them up a bit. Add the rest of the chilies, then sprinkle on a generous pinch each of chili powder, turmeric, garam masala, and salt.

2 Put the split rolls or bun on top, drizzle over a little more oil, and add another dusting of all the spices. Use a potato masher or similar-shaped implement to press down on the buns so they are smooshed into the egg. When it's fairly flat, flip it over and squash down again. Flip and squash a couple more times—the final result should be as flat as a pancake and crisping at the edges.

3 Cut the eggy pancake in half down the center. Fold each half into a sandwich, put on a plate, sprinkle with cilantro (coriander) and scallions (spring onions), and serve.

To Drink:

The Mustardy Mary

This recipe comes from my friend the food writer Kerstin Rodgers (aka Ms Marmite Lover), chef/patron of The Underground Restaurant and author of *Supper Club: Recipes and Notes from The Underground Restaurant*. When I asked her for permission to reproduce it here, she said "you need an après-shag cocktail?" which I thought was frankly a wonderful turn of phrase. The wholegrain mustard may sound a little leftfield but it works wonders and is a gorgeous twist on the traditional horseradish or Tabasco. So here it is, your après-shag cocktail.

Ingredients

Ice cubes

2 fl oz (50 ml) vodka

2 tbsp wholegrain mustard

1 pint (600 ml) tomato juice

Squeeze of fresh lemon juice

Freshly ground black pepper

Celery, to garnish

Serves 2

1 Fill a jug with ice and add the vodka. Add all the other ingredients and mix well. Divide between tall glasses and decorate each with a stick of celery, which doubles up as a stirrer.

2 This is all in the absence of either cold leftover pizza or curry, you understand, which are obviously the greatest hangover cures of all time.

Breakfast Lows

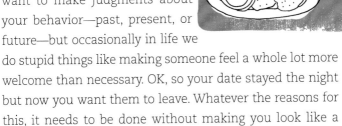

As ever in life, there is a flip side to this morning-after coin. I don't want to make judgments about your behavior—past, present, or future—but occasionally in life we do stupid things like making someone feel a whole lot more welcome than necessary. OK, so your date stayed the night but now you want them to leave. Whatever the reasons for this, it needs to be done without making you look like a mannerless chimp in the process. You have two options:

1 Canned Salvation

It's morning. You are hungover. You are looking for a way out of a rather demoralizing situation, preferably without losing any more self-respect by treating another person badly. That said, this requires forward planning and is therefore by its very nature a little bit on the wrong side of generally acceptable behavior. It requires that you anticipate the potential for this scenario to occur and you have therefore purchased in advance and stored diligently in the cupboard a couple of cans of... all-day breakfast. (US readers: I have been informed that this canned culinary disaster is not available in your obviously superior country. However, I have heard rumors of something called canned corned beef hash and I would advise giving it a go.)

Few pre-prepared foods can be as disgusting as all-day breakfast in a can (ADBIAC), surely? Let's break it down: beans, sausages, mushrooms, eggs, and, memorably, in one brand, "mini scotch eggs," the whole lot in "tasty tomato sauce." I've been a student, many times in fact, and I'm glad to say I've never stooped so low—and I've been pretty low. I once ate a piece of pizza that had been, albeit briefly, in the bin. I know. I actually consider the ADBIAC to be a worse offense. I had to go out and buy a can in order to write this.

I have now smelt the farty guff, as constrained, reclaimed protein is exposed to air once more. I have listened to the slow "plop, blip" as the homogeneous mass reheats in a pan, its viscous sauce threatening and reminiscent of the Bog of Eternal Stench in the film *Labyrinth*. The components are somewhat hard to identify, both visually and by scent. The aroma is that of baby farts, vinegar, and gas with, weirdly, a hint of cotton candy. It tastes like… I dunno, I couldn't bring myself to do it. Sorry. Serving this the morning after should do the trick, basically. If you want to really speed things along, I'd suggest eating it straight from the can, with your hands, in your underwear. Job done.

2 Gross Them Out

There is another method, of course, and that is to go down the road of offering food that is just wildly inappropriate for the hungover person. By this I mean, of course, something that is healthy, or even vaguely healthy. In fact, if you truly want to get rid of someone then I'd suggest giving them something **REALLY** healthy. My friend Veronica (not her real name) told me a story of how her wonderful boyfriend went through a health-food phase and once brought a selection of "sprouted things" to her sickbed as she lay, festering, dreaming of Diet Coke and bacon. A bowl of alfalfa sprouts and a piece of dry toast should do it.

Scrambled Lamb's Brains

Now I'm thinking about it, my mind is truly whirring with the terrible possibilities of using food to eject someone from your house. Got time to nip out to the butchers? Great. If your date doesn't get the hint and leave while you're gone then I suggest whipping up this little number upon your return. Warning: some people may actually enjoy this. But brains are the one bit of an animal I've never been able to eat. Anything else I can have a go at, but brains really gross me out and I suspect this is the same for a lot of other people. I kind of hope it is, actually. I'm supposed to be the food writer here; I can't have hungover people showing me up.

Ingredients

Butter, for frying

½ small onion, chopped

1 lamb's brain, carefully rinsed

3 eggs

A few sage leaves, chopped

Toast, to serve

Salt and freshly ground black pepper

Serves 2

1 Add a good knob of butter to a medium-hot frying pan and gently soften the onion for a few minutes.

2 Add the brain and stir around the pan gently so that it starts to break up into smaller clumps.

3 Crack in the eggs and carefully move them around the pan so that they cook and scramble together with the brains. Season with salt and pepper.

4 Once the eggs are almost cooked, stir in the chopped sage and remove from the heat. Serve on toast.

CHAPTER three

The Drunk Date

Post Pub Munchies

Ahhh, the romance! You've been out for a few drinks. OK, you've been in the pub for hours and are now both utterly hosed. It's the first time you've been properly drunk together, and you need something to soak it all up. Problem is, it's late and you're unprepared, which means it's going to be a convenience store job. **NO PROBLEM**.

Never have I been more of an expert in my field. Well, not since I wrote the bit about hangover cures anyway. OK, so this isn't going to be particularly sophisticated, but that doesn't really matter at this point. Drunk food is about finding that spot and hitting it. It is, yet again, about survival. You're probably hankering after a pizza or fried chicken, but **DON'T DO IT**. This is much cheaper, more fun and, well, this book is called *Cook Your Date Into Bed*, not *Take Your Date For Fried Chicken*, so here we are. Suck it up.

Your date will be amazed at the fact you can rustle up something so tasty from ingredients purchased from the late-night liquor store. They'll be impressed that you can rustle up anything at all that isn't baked beans on toast. All it will take is a quick dash around the aisles, dodging unsavory characters and squinting under flickering strip lighting, and you'll be set. If you're really lucky, you might get to order everything through one of those little hatches. Sounds appealing, huh? Bear with me.

Pimp My Instant Noodles, Yo! *finger whip*

OK, so what you're going to do is get some of those little blocks of dried noodles that cost like, nothing or whatever, the ones with the little sachets of dubious powder, and you're going to pimp 'em. What I mean is you're going to put loads of little extras on top and elevate those noodles until they're king of the goddamn hood, blud! What follows is a list of noodle-pimpage ingredients stocked by the finest convenience stores across the globe:

Scallions (spring onions): These are ESSENTIAL. Finely slice the green parts and use them to garnish the noodles.

Eggs: You can soft-boil, poach, or fry these, and serve on top. You can even poach the egg in the noodle broth if you're feeling fly.

Soy or fish sauce: A nice hit of umami.

SPAM: I dunno how you feel about the famous chopped pork and ham in a can, but if you're that way inclined you can fry a couple of slices and serve on top. Now don't go doubting my cooking credentials: in China they properly love SPAM, and that's serious noodle territory. You might want to find out where your date stands first, though.

Chili flakes or **hot sauce:** Makes even the blandest food taste considerably more exciting.

Fresh herbs: Basically, if you've got any fresh cilantro (coriander) knocking about then you've struck noodle-pimping gold.

Sesame or **chili oil**.

Baby spinach leaves: Just stir 'em in and they'll wilt down.

Sliced steak or chicken: Leftovers love noodles.

Shrimp (prawns): Just heat them through briefly in the noodle water. Add a wedge of lime to serve.

Pimp Skills

If you're a beginner, I suggest pimping with an egg and a dash of hot sauce, then adding a few drops of sesame oil, some chopped cilantro, and scallions. Once you've pimped, though, there's no going back. Just a warning. Pimped noodles will be creeping into your daytime repertoire. They're stealthy like that.

The Juiciest Lucy

Sometimes one needs to resort to methods that are a little, erm, "creative," in order to achieve the desired result. This burger makes one hell of a mess during eating and there's only one way to deal with the mess on those clothes. The "Juicy Lucy" is so called because the burger patty itself is stuffed with cheese, which oozes out from the center once bitten into. One word of warning, however: do let them cool down a little before eating; melted cheese burns are not sexy. The burgers can be (and are probably best) prepared before you head to the pub, but don't season them until you start cooking, as this will adversely affect the texture of the meat.

A Hot Beef Injection

Homemade burgers taste awesome, shop-bought versions taste like "meh." No brainer.

Ingredients

14 oz (400 g) ground rump steak, or ground beef of your choice; you want about 20% fat if possible. Get a butcher to grind it for you.

2 thick slices blue cheese (Roquefort, or if you don't like blue cheese, any cheese that melts), for filling

2 tbsp vegetable oil

2 slices cheese (Cheddar or—my preference—filthy, slappy processed cheese), for topping

2 seeded burger buns

½ red onion, thinly sliced

Shredded iceberg lettuce

2 dill pickles, sliced

Tomato ketchup

American-style yellow mustard

Salt and freshly ground black pepper

Serves 2

1 Divide the meat into two balls, and then in half once more. Take a piece of plastic wrap (cling film) and lay it out flat on a work surface. Place one of the balls of meat on top and lay another sheet of plastic wrap on top. Use something heavy like a skillet to flatten the ball of meat into a circle.

2 Carefully remove the plastic wrap from the top of the meat and repeat the process with the other three balls.

3 Take a slice of filling cheese and place it in the center of one of the patties. Lay another patty on top.

4 Repeat to make a second burger. Make sure to pinch down the edges of each burger to seal the two halves together and stop the cheese from leaking out during cooking. Pat the edges of each burger inwards slightly to form a flat side, rather than a pinched edge. At this point they can be refrigerated.

5 Get your burgers out of the refrigerator 30–60 minutes before cooking, if possible. Heat a skillet over a medium heat and add the vegetable oil. Season the outside of the burgers liberally with salt and pepper. Add a burger to the pan and cook for approximately 2–3 minutes, then flip over and top with one of the cheese slices.

6 Splash a tablespoon of water into the pan, then cover and cook for 2–3 minutes. Remove from the pan and place the burger onto the bottom half of a burger bun. Add onion, lettuce, pickles, and sauces (plenty of sauce—remember the motivation here). Add the top of the bun. Repeat with the second burger.

Song Suggestion: *Ignition* by R Kelly. "It's the freakin' weekend baby, I'm a gonna have me some fun."

CHAPTER four

The Movie Date

Secret Movie Snacks

I can't see the point of taking a date to the movies, you can't even talk during the film. Well, you **CAN**, but everyone will hate you. It's bloody antisocial if you ask me, and as I'm not 14 any more, the idea of sitting at the back with a boy's arm around me is repellent. I want to sit halfway down, because at the back, there will be a load of teenagers with their arms around each other, **OR WORSE**. The idea of teens getting intimate is just gross. You know this, because you've been one. The only reason we actually go to the movies with other people is so we can discuss the film later.

Anyway, I know people will continue to behave in this frankly baffling manner and so I provide here solutions to one major arsebag of a problem, the fact that movie food is rough. Popcorn is fine, although I've had more than one tiff with a server who refused to give me half salty, half sweet. **WHAT DIFFERENCE DOES IT MAKE, THEY'RE THE SAME PRICE**. The rest, though, is just rubbish, generic, boring.

Dessert on the Down Low

Imagine, if you will, that you are on a movie date and when you sit down your date whips out secret movie snacks. These homemade treats will absolutely kick the ass of anything the movie theater is selling. Plus your date actually made them. That's cool. That's fun. That's going to earn mega bonus points.

Chocolate Honeycomb Mousse in Jars

I am in no way trying to be trendy by making these in jars; it simply makes them easy to transport. And no, you can't just buy a Crunchie bar. Cheeky sod. Homemade honeycomb is really easy to make, not to mention dramatic. That's some mad shit going on right there. You'll see what I mean after you've made it.

To make the honeycomb

Ingredients

1 tbsp vegetable oil, for greasing the tin

4 tbsp light corn (golden) syrup

½ cup (100 g) superfine (caster) sugar

1½ tsp bicarbonate of soda

Serves 2 sugar fiends, most likely a lot more

Start with the honeycomb. Grease a high-sided cake tin (an 8 x 12 in [20 x 30 cm] one would be a good size) with the oil by wiping it all around with a piece of paper towel. Put the light corn (golden) syrup and sugar in a pan over a medium-high heat and let it all bubble up furiously. DO NOT STIR IT.

2 Once all the sugar has melted and the mixture is a lovely golden-brown color, whisk in your bicarbonate of soda. See? BATSHIT MENTAL. Turn out the frothy foaming mass into the tin and allow to cool.

To make the mousse

Ingredients

100 g milk chocolate (at least 30% cocoa solids)

2 eggs, separated

70 ml double cream

1 Half-fill a pan with water and bring to the boil, then reduce to a gentle simmer. Break up the chocolate and put it in a glass or metal bowl. Set the bowl over the simmering water, making sure the bottom of the bowl does not touch the water. Melt the chocolate gently, stirring occasionally. Remove the bowl from the heat and let the chocolate cool for 3 minutes, then stir in the egg yolks.

2 Whip the cream to soft peaks and fold it into the chocolate and egg mixture. Whisk the egg whites until stiff and then fold them into the mixture. Break the honeycomb into chunks and fold almost all of it into the mousse, then decant into the jars. Sprinkle the final pieces of honeycomb on top. Seal the jars and chill for at least 4 hours.

3 If it's a particularly hot day, or a long journey to the movie theater, then you might want to consider using a cool bag… and DON'T FORGET SPOONS.

To Drink:

Secret Thermos Hot Buttered Rum Cocktail

This recipe comes courtesy of my friend Felix Cohen, maker of incredibly classy cocktails and founder of The Manhattans Project bar. It is, quite simply, one of the dreamiest cocktails around. It's pure silk for the throat, soul, and mind. I mean, focus on the words... HOT BUTTERED RUM. If you're not in love with that combination, there's no hope for you. You'll need a thermos and two plastic cups (or proper glasses if you like—I'll allow it). Oh, and something to decant the rum into... they're not likely to be tolerant of you blatantly carrying a huge bottle of booze.

Ingredients

4 cups (1 liter) apple juice

1 stick (125 g) butter, diced

6 tbsp light corn (golden) syrup

1½ tbsp (25 ml) molasses (treacle)

1 tsp ground allspice

Approximately 1 cup (250 ml) golden rum (Felix uses Santa Teresa Anejo)

Cinnamon sticks, to serve

Serves 2, several times

1. Heat the apple juice in a pan over a medium heat. Stir in the diced butter, a little at a time. Once melted, stir in the light corn (golden) syrup and molasses (treacle). Once everything is well mixed, add the allspice. The temperature you're aiming for is about 175°F (80°C)—when you think it's about right, decant the buttery apple mixture into your thermos and seal the lid.

2. Once safely ensconced in the movie theater, bust out your cups and the rum. Add a shot of rum to each cup and top up with the warm, buttery apple juice—you want about four parts butter mixture to one part rum. It's nice to serve this with a cinnamon stick in the glass, to use as a stirrer.

CHAPTER five

The Picnic Date

Rug Life

I can't think of picnics without thinking of that frankly rather brilliant quote from the actor Sir Ian McKellen. Well, not so much a formal quote but more of an eavesdropped titbit, apparently. It's filthy. And hilarious.

Sir Ian: "Do you know the difference between a quiche and a blow job?"

Good Looking Young Actor: "No."

Sir Ian: "Come on a picnic with me and I'll show you."

HA. That's a picnic date right there, no messing. I can get behind picnic dates in general. They take place in the daytime, for a start, which automatically makes them cooler and takes the pressure off somewhat. People expect a lot less from a daytime meal than they do from an evening one. Picnics also provide a neat little opportunity to show your fun, spontaneous side, being as they are weather-dependent. An invitation to a picnic can make you look really cool if you spring the idea, say, the evening before. This depends of course entirely on whether or not you already had something planned and on what those plans were. Canceling a tasting menu at Le Gavroche or the French Laundry, for example—the one that you said would be entirely your shout—is a mistake whatever the weather.

We've all done bad picnics. The impractical wicker basket that looks the part but has you huffing and heaving up and down hills and over streams. Heat rash. Rug and blanket burn. Hayfever. Insect bites. Squished cakes. Warm mayonnaise. Worst of all—**THE FORGOTTEN CORKSCREW**. This last dilemma sounds like some terrible fable or lesson, and to be fair, it is. Make that mistake once and you won't make it again, let me tell you.

Not putting you off picnics, am I? Hmm. Just pick a decent spot is all I'm saying. See that red ants' nest? Yeah, avoid that. See that crowd of young kids playing football? Stay the hell away. Oh, and always remember to avoid **NATIONAL FLYING ANT DAY**. You know it. Every single year it seems that every single flying ant in the entire world hatches out on the same damn day and they get everywhere. In hair, on faces, behind people's glasses... Keep bugs off the menu.

The Joy of Insects

Wasps in your sandwiches, ants in your sandwiches, sand in your sandwiches. Sandwiches. Actually, hang on. I must pause here to point out that I am very much pro-sandwich. I adore them, actually, to the point where I've even written a book on the subject. *Shameless plug* 101 *Sandwiches* features the best sandwich recipes from around the world and is out now, $18.95/£12.99. *Shameless plug ends* However, it is very easy to do them badly. Also, this just isn't really the time. This is not a picnic with your mate, or your sister, or your grandma. This is a date, and unless you're going to go balls out banger (see page 102) with fillings, it isn't really going to work. Even dainty, crustless, triangular, or finger sandwiches are a touch lame for a date situation. Finger sarnies at The Ritz is one thing, finger sarnies on a rug under a tree is... well, it's a little bit children's party.

For the first time in my life, I'm going to avoid sandwiches altogether. This cooking-to-impress lark is all about slinging curveballs and so that is what we shall do. We are going to be sophisticated. You are going to bake your own bread. You are going to put fruit and herbs on the top and eat it with cheese. It will be fabulous and you will immediately come across as someone who is grown up, has a fantastic palate, is a whizz in the kitchen, and is imaginative to boot.

Cherry Focaccia with Goats' Cheese

Homemade bread impresses everyone. Fact.

Ingredients

4 cups (500 g) strong white bread flour

2 x ¼-oz (7-g) sachets dried yeast

1 tsp sugar

2 tsp salt

2 tbsp olive oil, plus extra for drizzling

14 fl oz (400 ml) cold water

20 cherries, pitted

1 level tsp sea salt

1 tbsp roughly chopped rosemary

Firm, sharp goats' cheese (not the really soft, spreadable kind), to serve

Makes 2 loaves. Give one to your granny, she'll love it.

1 Put the flour, yeast, sugar, and salt into a bowl, making sure that the yeast and salt are on opposite sides of the bowl. Add the olive oil and water and bring together into a dough. Knead for 5 minutes to make a smooth, soft dough and then set aside in a lightly oiled bowl and leave to rise until doubled in size.

2 Once the dough has risen, divide it into two and flatten each piece out on a lightly oiled baking sheet. Leave to prove for 1 hour. Preheat the oven to 425°F/220°C/Gas 7.

3 Use your fingertips to make dimples on the top of the dough and push a cherry into each. Drizzle with a little olive oil and rub over the surface with your fingers, then sprinkle with the sea salt and rosemary, pressing it gently onto the dough. Bake in the preheated oven for 20 minutes.

4 To serve, tear pieces off the focaccia, rip open with your hands and stuff with a slice of goats' cheese. The sweet cherries and sharp cheese are a killer combination. Oh, hang on a minute… this is a sandwich, isn't it? Wow, I really am unstoppable.

Sweet Ting

I think it's time to get a bit silly with dessert. Enter the comedian of the dessert world: jelly. Yes, my American friends, jelly. We say jelly, you say jello; we say arse, you say fanny; we say fanny, you say... er, look it up.

Moving on, is there anything more ridiculous and childishly pleasing than a wobbly jelly? There is not. Move your mind away, if you will, from those blocks of dense, lurid concentrate we used to use as kids. Did you eat them "straight" too? Man, that was one concentrated hit of goodness knows what, but I'm not for a moment suggesting you buy a pack of that stuff and add boiling water. I am suggesting that you make a properly grown-up jelly with real fruit and everything, and by "everything" I mean booze. The fruit is going to be pomegranate, because it's a lovely grown-up flavor—both tart and sweet. Classy. It also has a wonderful, shocking, deeply purple color.

There are two ways to go with serving the jelly, depending on how committed you are to getting a laugh out of your date. The first is that you can simply pour the jelly into small glass jars and let it set there. It will be easy to transport and can be eaten straight from the jar with a spoon.

The second is more ambitious so obviously the way to go. You'll need to get hold of some small jelly molds (try online or in kitchen shops) and let your jelly set in them. Then, you need to take a flask of warm water to the picnic, plus a bowl and two plates. When you are ready to eat the jelly, pour some of the warm water into the bowl and let the mold sit in it for about 5 seconds (don't let the water touch the exposed jelly).

You can then turn it the right way up and try to ease it out onto the plate. You do this by just gently squeezing the sides of the mold. It should be relatively easy, actually. If it doesn't come out try dunking it in the water once more. Once you have it on the plate you can have maximum fun with the wobbling. Hold the side of the plate and move gently back and forth. The jelly will go wild with excitement. Comedy sound effects optional. If your date doesn't laugh at this, pack everything up and go home. Separately.

Pomegranate and Prosecco Jelly

It's tempting to see a garnish as optional. Don't—it makes all the difference when eating. Prep the pom seeds before you go out.

Ingredients

4 leaves gelatin

¾ cup (200 ml) pomegranate juice

2 tbsp superfine (caster) sugar

½ cup (100 ml) Prosecco

Pomegranate seeds, to serve

Crème fraîche, to serve

Makes 4. Eat the other two yourself or something.

1 Soak the gelatin leaves in a bowl of cold water for a few minutes, until they are soft. Heat the pomegranate juice and sugar together in a small pan until the sugar is dissolved.

2 Wring out any excess moisture from the gelatin leaves and add them to the pan; stir until the gelatin has dissolved. Remove the pan from the heat and lob in the Prosecco. You can now leave this to cool before pouring into your vessel of choice, be it jar (wimp!) or mold (hero!).

3 To serve the jello, either unscrew the jar lids and add a spoonful of crème fraîche and a sprinkle of pomegranate seeds (cop out) or unmold the jelly onto plates as described above and serve the crème fraîche alongside with pom seeds on top (winner!).

To Drink:

Tinto de Verano

This kick-ass drink is so perfect for summer it is actually painful. It hurts me on the inside with its overwhelming suitability for glugging in the sunshine. It is also truly a spot-on match for the cherry focaccia with goats' cheese. See how I look after you? Tinto de Verano is in fact nothing more than red wine and lemonade mixed together but oh! The joy! The name is Spanish, the literal translation being "red wine of summer." It's basically just a red wine spritzer, yet sounds really swanky. Perfecto. If you have never experienced fizzy red wine please let me enlighten you my friend because it is the freaking FUTURE. The fizz lightens it, and serving it slightly chilled does so even further. The lemonade adds sweetness, of course, and the whole combination is just one big refreshment bomb. Also, it's about a million times classier than sangria, which should be reserved for tacky tourist joints next to tat shops selling straw donkeys. Yeah, we've all done it, but this is the time to up your game. Tinto de Verano should be served chilled, for maximum refreshment. Take a cool bag or box with you for the ice.

Ingredients

Ice

1 bottle red wine (something like a basic Tempranillo will work well, and by "basic" I mean "quite cheap")

1½ cups (350 ml) sparkling lemonade (not the cloudy stuff)

Sparkling water (optional)

Lemon slices

Makes 6 drinks

1 | Fill each glass with ice and then fill about two-thirds with red wine. Top up with lemonade.

2 | If it's too sweet, you may want to add some sparkling water. Garnish with a lemon slice and serve.

Song suggestion: *Black Gold of The Sun* by Rotary Connection.

OK, so let's recap. You've got the food and booze ready, so don't screw it up by forgetting all the other stuff. Here is a list of things you really don't want to forget, because we haven't had a list for a while and it's making me twitchy.

1 THE CORKSCREW

2 Glasses

3 Cutlery

4 Plates, bowls, and so on, for each of your separate dishes

5 A rug

6 Maybe a couple of cushions?

7 Cool bag/box with ice in it

8 Oh, the actual food and drink

9 A bag to clear up any mess

10 Some mini speakers and music if you're really fly and you're going to be sufficiently far enough away from other people not to be a massive chump

CHAPTER SIX

The BBQ Date

Where There's Smoke, There's Fire (and Food)

The BBQ date is practically perfect, particularly for a first date, because it does not require a constant one-on-one situation; there's plenty (hopefully) of other people there to take the heat off, yet there are opportunities to talk, unlike the shitty movie date which I still don't get but nevertheless felt the need to write about. Provided you do your prepping beforehand, and you know how to handle the barbecue properly, you're going to seriously impress your date. And yes, I am going to tell you what to prep and how to handle the barbecue properly.

How you approach the barbecue is likely going to be highly dependent on whether you are a UK or a US resident, and as this book is published in both countries, I feel I need to explain myself further. In the US, there is a long history of barbecue and it means, in general, long, slow cooking. It means smoking, it means regional specialties, it means pit masters and briskets and smoke rings and Texas and Kansas style. In short, it means a whole lot more in the US than it has in the UK, until very recently. In the UK—again the caveat "until recently" applies here—barbecue has been thought of as what our American friends would term "grilling," that is, cooking over direct heat. Now, things are different and we have some fantastic restaurants and chefs who champion "proper" barbecue but oh, **OH**, the horrors of the old-school, novice British barbecue. I refuse to rake too deeply over those coals (sorry) but I will just allude to the pathetic examples of grilling that many people may have had to endure at some point or other in their lives: blackened sausages that are raw in the middle, the odd sad-looking burger, a mountain of pappy cheap buns that stick to the roof of your mouth, and perhaps a token side of mayo-based coleslaw. I allude to this purely so I can give a major **"FUCK YOU!"** to people who think that the British still barbecue like that. Sure, there are some people doing that in the privacy of their own back yards, and that's fine—they don't care about food, just leave them to it—but I am not having any sweeping generalizations happening and I am certainly not having you being any part of them. You can cook a kick-ass barbecue and you damn well will.

Comes up for air OK so you're not going to be entering the next American Royal (that's a barbecue competition, folks; a barbecue competition for which you first have to win other barbecue competitions in order to be invited to take part), but you're not going to go anywhere near any pre-prepped burgers or sausages, either. I mean it. I'll get angry. Your date deserves better. You deserve better. The barbecue deserves better. **THE WORLD DEFINITELY DESERVES BETTER.**

Get the Gear

Which brings me to the subject of equipment. You need a half-decent barbecue to make this work, there's no point in pretending otherwise. If you're using a flimsy-wimsy, teeny-weeny thing that you picked off a supermarket shelf, then I advise you, strongly, to choose another chapter. This is not the date for you. If you considered, even for one nanosecond, that you might just use one of those throwaway disposable jobbies, then I assume you are just having a laugh, right? **RIGHT?!** I have a crazy look in my eyes right now. That is not a barbecue. That is nothing even approaching a barbecue. If I see it I will smash it. You cannot create anything impressive on that piece of shit. Ever. You will also find it impossible to feed more than one person.

All you need is a half-decent kettle barbecue. If you don't have one, then maybe borrow one? I don't want to patronize you here. You know about borrowing things, right? You know about buying things? I leave these tricky decisions entirely up to you.

Come On Baby Light My Fire

Now we have all that out of the way, it's time to talk about setting up your barbecue. We're going to employ a method here that is known as the "two zone." All it means is that your coals are going to be on one side of the barbecue, the reason being that this allows the heat to circulate inside. You will be able to control the heat much more effectively, which means you will cook the food much better, without burning it, and without worrying about it still being raw in the middle. You don't want your date to remember you as "the one who gave me botulism." One of the best ways to light coals is to use a starter chimney, but if you have one of those then you probably don't need me to tell you how to set up a barbecue, so let's assume you don't. Place two firelighters on one side of the bottom of the barbecue and build up coals around them (you still need to light the firelighters, so don't cover them completely). Light the firelighters. The coals will soon catch. There will be smoke at first but don't freak out because that's just moisture coming off the charcoal. Once the coals are lit, put the rack on. You now need to wait. You must, I repeat MUST wait until the coals are covered with a layer of light ash before you start cooking. The coals are ready at this point and not before.

Bust Out That BBQ

OK, barbecue lecture over. Here is a menu for you. Let's get to it.

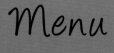

MAIN COURSE:

Kick-ass Koftas with Mint Yogurt and Smoky Eggplant Sauce

"Dirty" Barbecue Veg with Lemon and Herb Dressing

DESSERT:

Redneck Ice Cream Sandwiches

TO DRINK:

Bad Juice

Kick-ass Koftas with Mint Yogurt and Smoky Eggplant Sauce

A touch of Middle-Eastern magic for your grill.

Ingredients

1 lb 2 oz (500 g) ground lamb

½ onion

1 tsp ground coriander

2 tsp ground cumin

1 tsp chili flakes, to taste

6 metal skewers for cooking the kebabs

Salt and freshly ground black pepper

Makes 6 koftas, but you can easily scale this up

To make the koftas

1 Start the koftas a few hours before you want to eat them. Put the ground lamb into a large bowl. Grate the onion into it. Yes, I'm afraid you do have to grate it, otherwise you will end up with chunks of raw onion in your koftas (yes, even after they have been cooked). Just do it. Add the ground coriander, cumin, chili flakes, and a generous amount of salt and pepper.

2 Now, you need to get your hands in there and mix really well. In fact, you need to work that meat quite a bit, almost as if you were kneading bread. The reason for this is that it firms up the mixture and it will save you a headache later on.

3 Divide the meat into six and press around the skewers. Refrigerate for at least 2 hours.

4 Around 40 minutes before you want to serve the koftas, light the barbecue as described above. When the coals are ready, add the koftas to the side of the rack without coals underneath. Cook them there, turning them regularly, say every few minutes or so, for about 15 minutes, or until cooked through.

Ingredients

8 tbsp natural yogurt

Small handful of mint leaves, finely shredded

Juice of ½ lemon

Ingredients

4 large eggplants (aubergines)

1 tbsp finely chopped flat-leaf parsley

Juice of ½ lemon

Salt and freshly ground black pepper

To make the yogurt sauce

Mix the yogurt with the finely shredded mint leaves, plus the juice of half a lemon. Season the yogurt with salt and pepper to taste, mix well, and refrigerate until your koftas are ready to eat.

To make the eggplant sauce

There are two ways to approach the smoky eggplant. You can either a) cook them indoors so you can have the sauce ready in advance, or b) cook them on the barbecue for extra smokiness. Whether or not you choose to do the latter depends on the size of your barbecue and how happy you feel about starting them off before you start cooking the koftas, and making the sauce while the koftas finish cooking, so that everything is ready at the same time. No one likes a cold kofta.

2 In either case, prick the eggplants all over with a fork. If cooking indoors, place them directly on the gas flame of a stove with the heat on low and move them about every now and again until they are blackened all over and collapsed.

Alternatively, place them on a baking sheet under a hot broiler (grill), turning every now and then until you get the same effect. If cooking on the barbecue, place them on the rack directly over the coals.

3 Once the eggplants are blackened, transfer to a plate. When cool enough to handle, scoop out the flesh from the inside, leaving behind the black skin (a few small bits are fine and will actually add to the flavor). Chop the flesh roughly and mix with the juice of the other lemon half, the chopped parsley, and some salt and pepper.

Ingredients

6 pitta breads

Salad leaves, such as watercress and arugula (rocket)

Salt and freshly ground black pepper

To serve

4 When the koftas are cooked, transfer to a plate while you briefly toast the pitta breads on the barbecue—this will take seconds each side, so do pay attention. Serve the toasted pittas with the koftas, smoky eggplant sauce, yogurt sauce, and salad leaves. You have made the most glorious barbecued kebabs. Well done!

"Dirty" Barbecue Veg with Lemon and Herb Dressing

Right, so cooking something "dirty" on the barbecue means actually cooking it directly in the coals. That's right. You'll be putting the stuff you are going to eat directly into the hot, burning, ash-covered coals and it will taste amazing when it's done. I learned about it from a guy I know called Marcus, who's a bit of a shit-hot barbecue chef as it happens so don't you knock it till you've tried it. It's possible to use this method to cook steaks and all sorts, but I think it works really nicely with vegetables. They also cook really fast, so you can do them at the same time as the meat. The end result is something that tastes really smoky and just a bit feral, in a good way.

Ingredients

1 red bell pepper

1 yellow or orange bell pepper

1 zucchini (courgette)

2 large red onions, peeled and quartered

2 whole green chilies

2 tbsp olive oil

1 large sprig of rosemary, leaves chopped

1 lemon, halved

1 clove of garlic, crushed

Salt and freshly ground black pepper

Serves 2

Put all the veg, including the chilies, in a large bowl and slosh in the olive oil. Add the chopped rosemary and some salt and pepper and give everything a good mix about. Remove the veg from the bowl and place directly into the coals. They will cook at different speeds, so keep an eye on them and turn them regularly using tongs. Don't fret about this, just trust your instincts. They need to have charred spots on the outside, and they need to feel softened but still retain some bite. I'd be surprised if you got this really wrong, so don't panic.

2 Squeeze the juice of half a lemon into the same bowl that you used to coat the vegetables with oil and rosemary. Add the clove of crushed garlic and some salt and pepper.

3 When the vegetables are all cooked, remove them from the coals. Allow the veg to cool enough that you can just about handle them without burning your fingers, then chop each piece up fairly small. Add them back to the bowl with the lemon dressing in and mix well—it's essential the veg is still warm at this point, it helps the flavors to develop. Add an extra splash of olive oil if required.

4 This can be served as a side dish or used as an accompaniment to any grilled meats—it is particularly nice in a wrap or pitta.

Redneck Ice Cream Sandwiches

Yee-haw! Time for dessert. For me, desserts are pointless unless they can raise a smile. That's the way to end a meal on a high, and I say that with confidence, as this ain't my first rodeo, if you catch my meaning. To make this a true redneck barbecue I guess we should have eaten roadkill as a main course, but it's a little bit hit-and-miss when it comes to sourcing. I think it's fun to eat something a little bit trashy at a barbecue. As long as the majority of the food has more substance, a silly dessert will be fun, rather than leaving your guests feeling internally violated. This is basically an ice cream sandwich, wearing a load

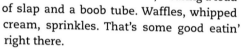

of slap and a boob tube. Waffles, whipped cream, sprinkles. That's some good eatin' right there.

You can also make judgments about your date based on whether or not they choose to use cutlery or decide to get in there with their hands. Personally I would be far more impressed with the latter. It's probably an indication of their sexual prowess. Or something.

Ingredients

Heavy (double) cream

1 frozen waffle per person

1–2 scoops of ice cream per person

Sugar sprinkles

Whip the heavy (double) cream. Toast a waffle, then add 1 or 2 scoops of ice cream. Fold in half, then top with a splodge of whipped cream and confetti of sugar sprinkles.

Song suggestion: *Sweet Home Alabama* by Lynyrd Skynyrd.

To Drink:

Bad Juice

This drink is inspired by a man who sells luridly colored drinks in the street in south London, where I live. He wheels a cart around which contains a huge block of ice, plus various unmarked bottles. "Come on, mon, come on and try some BAD JUICE!" He takes a plastic sandwich bag, shaves a load of ice and whacks it in, before squirting it with fluorescent jets of what looks like pure E numbers from bottles that clearly once contained ketchup. The result is a big ball of ice that Rainbow Brite would have been proud of. It's brilliant, obviously. The flavors are of the kind that cannot really be identified; they don't exist in nature, as fruits or otherwise, and are entirely artificial, yet wonderfully familiar. If you catch him on a really good day, however, rum gets involved. This is really, truly some bad, bad juice.

Ingredients

Crushed ice (try pulsing ice cubes in a blender)

1 measure white rum

1 measure overproof gold rum

Selection of luridly colored fruit-flavored soft drinks. You can't go too wrong if you just stick to fruit flavors. Try orangeade, limeade, a splash of ginger beer. GO CRAZY.

Serves 1

1 Put a handful of crushed ice into a glass, or if you're feeling really fly, into a sandwich bag.

2 Now it's time to get some color and flavor into that ice, so pour in a little of each of the soft drinks you have selected.

3 Next, add a modest splash each of the rums and give it a stir. Add a straw and serve.

Song suggestion:
Boom Shack A Lack
by Apache Indian.

CHAPTER seven

Aphrodisiacs

The Science Bit

What a load of bullshit. Well, so the evidence suggests. Unfortunately for my publishers, I'm also an academic, which means I am more than capable of assessing the actual body of evidence for certain widely held assumptions—in this case, that certain foods have aphrodisiac qualities. Oysters, chocolate, figs. They all supposedly make you horny. Science says this is more than likely rubbish, and yet I have included them in this book. Why? Well, because what scientific enquiry has genuinely found evidence for is the power of suggestion. Tell someone that some thing will make them feel a certain way and there's a high chance it will. A classic placebo effect. And why not take advantage of this phenomenon?

Aphrodisiac ingredients were first sought-after as remedies for sexual difficulties and anxieties. You could've guessed that. Food as medicine was an attractive option in the absence of, well, any medicine. The methods of identification were brilliantly scientific; I've heard that the Aztecs selected the avocado, for example, because the way the fruits hang in pairs on the tree resembles testicles. **IT'S A SIGN**! They named the tree "Ahuacuat," which translates as "testicle tree." Nice. Sometimes I wonder if it really is just the case that supposed aphrodisiac ingredients look a bit rude. Consider figs. What is it about figs, exactly? I can't put my finger on it but they're definitely hinting at something. Filthbags. Then there are the oysters, which are just blatantly suggestive of inside bits and private places; the texture most certainly does not help. Asparagus. Obvious, that one. The green variety is bad enough but the white? Obscene. Grip a spear of white asparagus in the wrong way and you're in all sorts of trouble.

It's also just a bit of a coincidence that most of these supposed libido-enhancers happen to taste nice. What an almighty piece of good luck it is that the ingredients decided upon by man as beneficial to the body and mind also just happen to taste really delicious: chocolate (a foodstuff so tasty that people apparently become "chocoholics"), figs, strawberries, pomegranates, apricots, and avocados— some of the most decadent fruits in existence. Asparagus is one of the most prized seasonal vegetables of all. Sweet serendipity.

Hang on a moment, though, what is this? Deer penis, you say? Ooh, lovely. Hippocrates was a fan, I've heard. And what about the Chinese? Traditional medicine prescribes all manner of penises. Bull's penis, turtle penis, tiger penis. Penis, penis, penis. Sounds like a load of bollocks to me.

The Food of Love (or Lust)

OK, so here we go; these are your "aphrodisiac" recipes. I've provided a handy pointer to the aphrodisiac ingredients at the start of each recipe. Feel free to pass the information on to your date, if you like. It depends on how comfortable you are with them knowing of your intentions.

Menu

STARTER:

Steamed Asparagus with
Crabby Vinaigrette

MAIN COURSE:

Sizzling Fish with Chili, Ginger, and
Scallion (Spring Onion)

DESSERT:

Drunken Baked Figs

TO DRINK:

Boozy Mexican Hot Chocolate

Steamed Asparagus with Crabby Vinaigrette

A nice little starter that is impressive yet very easy to make. I've made this sound a bit silly by calling it "crabby" when it is, in fact, really rather elegant.

Aphrodisiac count: ❤
(asparagus)

Ingredients

1 bunch asparagus (about 8–10 spears)

2 tbsp lemon juice

4 tbsp olive oil (not extra virgin)

Pinch of cayenne pepper

Pinch of white pepper

1 tsp capers, rinsed and chopped

3½ oz (100 g) fresh white crabmeat (you can buy this from fishmongers or in little pots in posh delis)

Salt

Serves 2

1 Remove the woody ends from the asparagus. This can be done by holding each spear at both ends and bending gently until the end snaps off. Bring a medium-sized pan of water to the boil, add the asparagus, and simmer for 3 minutes. Drain and refresh under cold water to stop them from cooking any further.

2 Make the vinaigrette by whisking together the lemon juice and olive oil until emulsified. Add the cayenne pepper, white pepper, and just a little salt. Stir in the capers and crabmeat. Taste and add more salt or pepper if required.

3 To serve, divide the asparagus spears between two plates and spoon half the dressing over each, making sure you distribute the crabmeat evenly.

Sizzling Fish with Chili, Ginger, and Scallion

It's a bit of a shameless party piece, this one. The delicate fish is topped with a garnish of hot oil, chili, and ginger, which sizzles and steams, creating the most incredible fragrance. I'd recommend adding the garnish at the table for maximum effect. Serve with plain white rice and lightly cooked greens such as pak choi.

Aphrodisiac count: ❤❤ (ginger and chili)

Ingredients

Ice

2 scallions (spring onions), green parts only, cut into thin strips

1 red chili, cut into thin strips (up to you whether or not to remove the seeds)

2 x 5½-oz (160-g) fillets of sea bass (or use sea bream)

1-in (2.5-cm) piece of ginger, peeled and cut into very thin matchsticks

1 tbsp soy sauce

1 tbsp groundnut oil

2 tsp sesame oil

A few small sprigs fresh cilantro (coriander), leaves picked

Salt

Serves 2

1 OK, so here's a nifty trick. To make your scallion (spring onion) oil thing even more dramatic and brilliant, you're going to use a bit of kitchen magic. Fill a bowl with water and add a good handful or two of ice.

2 Now throw the scallion and chili strips into it and in 15 minutes or so they will all have curled up. This will make the finished dish look extra impressive. Drain and dry on paper towels.

3 Meanwhile, put the fish fillets on a plate and sprinkle with the ginger pieces. Pour over the soy sauce and let sit for 15 minutes. Set a steamer basket over a pan of simmering water and place the fish fillets inside, leaving the ginger strips on the fish. Sprinkle over a pinch of salt. Steam for 7 minutes, then turn off the heat while you prepare the oil.

4 Heat the groundnut and sesame oils in a small pan and add the chili strips; cook for about 1 minute. Place the fish fillets on a plate in the middle of the table and scatter over the spring onions. Pour the chili oil over the fish to impressive effect and finish by scattering over a few cilantro leaves.

Figs

I really wanted to make a figgy pudding for this recipe, but that was until I googled it and realized exactly what it was. Man, that is one unsexy dessert. A big blob on a plate. A nap-inducing ball of stodge, reminiscent of Christmas pudding and—I think you'll agree—not at all the sort of thing we should be aiming for. Then I just started agonizing over the damn figs, thinking about what I'd do with them if I had some, right now. The answer was, every time, "just eat them." Not helpful. There must be other ways I like to eat figs? Well, I do like them baked into a loaf of bread, but let's face it, that's a massive faff and would possibly make it look like you were trying a touch too hard. Then I remembered the time a friend and I stuffed them with cheese and wrapped them in Parma ham. Then I remembered it's not 2001 any more. That's a good little rule for cooking date food, FYI: never, **EVER**, wrap anything in Parma ham. Definitely never stuff anything with cheese and **THEN** wrap it in Parma

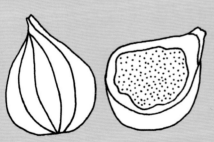

ham, particularly if that thing to be stuffed is a chicken breast. It's just terribly unimaginative. Sorry if that's something you like to cook.

The Notorious F.I.G.

So back to the figs. I did consider a tart but then it's just, you know, making pastry, and even though that's not particularly hard I just don't know where you're at with the cooking. I have no idea what you might be capable of when it comes to kitchen fuck-uppery. I have lived with people who have made some staggering errors in the kitchen. There was the woman who had never cooked pasta before, so she just put the whole plastic bag of penne directly into boiling water. I also witnessed a man putting a pizza in the oven, still in its plastic wrapping. I shit you not. Now I am not suggesting for a moment that you are that incompetent, I'm just saying I don't know what I'm dealing with here and I am 100% on your side; in other words, I don't want you to screw anything up, which is what led to the rejection of the pastry idea. If you want to go the extra mile, or, as I have eloquently put it, go "balls out banger," then you need to hop to the next chapter. If you want to stick right here, thanks very much, then it's time to get down with baking some figs.

Drunken Baked Figs

And so to our aphrodisiac dessert. Figs are most excellent once baked and are really simple to make, merely requiring some slinging of stuff into a roasting tin and whacking into the oven. I have, of course, made them "drunken" because I appear to be styling myself as the new Keith Floyd, something that is happening alarmingly naturally.

Aphrodisiac count: ❤❤❤ (figs, honey, nutmeg, and booze)

Ingredients

6 ripe figs

2 tbsp honey

Splash of brandy, Masala, or Madeira

4 tbsp 0% fat Greek yogurt (not trying to be healthy; it's that the acidity of 0% yogurt works better with the very sweet fruit)

Zest of ½ orange

Light grating of nutmeg (nutmeg is prized as an aphrodisiac, but don't get overexcited and start necking them whole; it's also a powerful hallucinogenic in large quantities. You'll be completely off your tits, and not in a good way)

Serves 2

1 Preheat the oven to 350°F/180°C/Gas 4.

2 Cut the figs in half lengthwise and arrange them in a shallow baking dish, close together. Attempt to evenly distribute the honey over them, followed by your booze of choice. Add a light grating of nutmeg to each fig, then cover and bake in the oven for approximately 20 minutes, or until softened.

3 Mix together the yogurt and orange zest and serve with the figs.

To Drink:

Boozy Mexican Hot Chocolate

Proper hot chocolate is pretty glorious and not really something that people bother to make too often, therefore catapulting it into the treat category. This is the kind of thing you could make for a "sofa date," by which I mean you have ended up watching a film together at home, or something similar. It's a lot more sociable than the movies, that's for sure...

Aphrodisiac count: ♥♥ (chocolate, chili, plus a booze bonus)

Ingredients

½ cup (125 ml) water

4 oz (125 g) dark chocolate, broken into small pieces

1 tbsp superfine (caster) sugar

½ tsp vanilla extract

Pinch of chili powder

Pinch of salt

2 shots dark rum (or whatever you prefer; Cointreau also works well)

2 cinnamon sticks

Serves 2

1 Place all the ingredients except the cinnamon sticks and rum in a pan and place over a medium heat, stirring constantly. The chocolate is ready when everything is dissolved and it is hot but not boiling.

2 Pour the rum (or your choice of alcohol) into mugs, followed by the chocolate mixture. To serve, add a cinnamon stick to each mug; this can be used every now and then to stir up any chocolate that has dared to settle on the bottom.

CHAPTER eight

Balls Out Banger

Go Big or Go Home

To go balls out banger. I fear this may be a phrase used solely by me and my mates. I can't remember where it came from, but I feel I should credit my friend Lizzie. So, to clarify, it means to "go for it," to "push the boat out," to basically go at something like you damn well mean it. We often use the phrase in reference to the way we have approached an evening out when said evening was particularly messy. You get the idea.

This is a chapter for those of you who want to make a really special effort to impress. You want to tackle some more serious cooking, possibly using expensive ingredients. This is a well-trodden path when it comes to impressing a date, and yet it is also a dangerous one with many potential pitfalls, not least that you will screw up the cooking and look like a total muppet. If you've got the nerve though (and the cash), then go for it, I say. If you pull it off then the meal could be spectacular and you are pretty much guaranteed to impress your date. Actually, even if you do fluff it, your date should still appreciate the effort, and if they don't, then they can hit the road anyway, let's face it.

A Meal to Remember

What I've done here is taken cheesy dinner-party classics and made them, frankly, bang up to date and awesome. Certain dishes became hugely popular for good reason, but then fell out of favor because they were done to death and so became clichéd. The essence—oh crikey, I can't use a word like "essence" and still be taken seriously—erm, the core… no. The foundation—sod it—the foundation of these dishes is a sound one and they really lend themselves to a bit of gussying up into something really impressive. They just need a little modernization. A little more balls to their banger, if you will.

This lobster will be cooked from fresh, and yes, that does mean putting a live lobster into the pot. Well, two actually. Make sure your pots are big enough to hold the lobsters BEFORE you start cooking. I speak from bitter experience. It is generally agreed by animal welfare groups that the acceptable thing is to put your lobsters into the freezer two hours before you want to cook them, which sort of sends them to sleep so they don't thrash about when you put them in the water. The evidence for them actually feeling any pain is inconclusive, but if there is any doubt at all, I say go with the freezer method. I always do. Anyway, no one wants thrashing lobsters, it's a headfuck. Also, I know it sounds really obvious but I'll say it anyway—those elastic bands are round the claws for a reason so for goodness' sake do not remove them until the lobsters are cooked.

Oh, and finally, I want to say that although this may look like a bit of a faff, cooking lobster is actually really easy. It's just a case of knowing what to do.

Menu

STARTER:

Lobster Cocktail

MAIN COURSE:

Duck à la Pamplemousse

DESSERT:

Profiteroles with Chocolate Sauce
and Cherries

TO DRINK:

Champagne Cocktails

Lobster Cocktail

This is like a shrimp cocktail but better because it contains lobster, see? And there won't be any marie rose sauce, either (while I am partial to marie rose, we don't want to evoke any 1970s dinner-party vibes).

Ingredients

2 live lobsters

Serves 2

To cook the lobster

1 Put your lobsters in the freezer for 2 hours before you want to cook them.

2 Bring a really huge pan of water to the boil or, more likely, two large pans. Plunge the lobsters in and cover with lids. Cook them for 3 minutes then turn the heat off and leave for 7 minutes longer. Remove the lobsters and set aside to cool.

To extract the meat

1 When cool enough to handle, extract the meat—make sure you keep the shell pieces. I do this using a hammer, nutcracker, and, erm, a chopstick—you may have the correct implements. Basically just get it all out using the following method:

2 Twist the body away from the head and claws.

3 Turn the tail on its side and press down until the shell cracks. Turn it so the shell is facing down and then push outward on opposite sides so

the tail splits open. You can now remove the meat. There is a dark vein running along the back of the tail, which you will find by running a knife down the center of the lobster. Remove and discard this. Give the tail a wash, rinsing away any green bits inside (don't freak out, as this is normal, but you don't want them in your dish).

4 Twist off both the arms of the lobster (the limbs with the massive claws on the ends). You will see that there is a claw and two knuckle pieces—separate these.

5 To remove the meat from the two knuckle pieces, just get something thin like a skewer, a chopstick, or the end of a spoon and push through until the meat comes out. For the claw, wiggle the smaller pincer and see if there is any meat inside; if there is, pull it out. For the large piece, you need to crack it, using lobster crackers, nutcrackers, a hammer, whatever. Remove the meat inside.

6 Twist off each of the little legs underneath and use a rolling pin to remove the meat from each. Roll the pin over the leg, rolling away from your body, and the meat will come out of the end. Stop before you get to the end of the leg so as not to roll bits of shell into the meat.

7 Very roughly chop the lobster meat, keeping some nice big pieces, and set aside in a bowl.

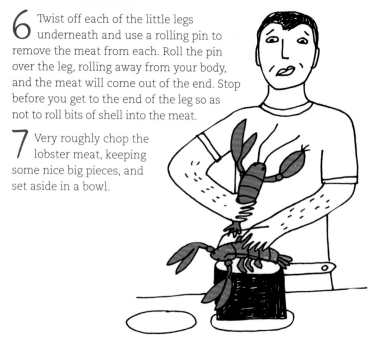

Ingredients

Vegetable oil

½ small onion, finely chopped

1 stick celery, finely chopped

To make the bisque

1 Discard the head of the lobster, then put all the other reserved shell pieces into a large clean pan with a splash of vegetable oil.

2 Add the finely chopped onion and celery. Fry over a medium-high heat for a few minutes, stirring occasionally.

3 Add about 4 cups (1 liter) of water and bring to the boil, then reduce the heat and simmer for 30 minutes.

4 Strain the liquid into a clean pan and then reduce for about 30 minutes, or until the level of the bisque is around ¾ in (2 cm) above the base of the pan. You'll know it's ready when it tastes like an intense, kick-ass flavor bomb. You don't need a huge quantity as you'll be adding it to the mayo.

Ingredients

2 egg yolks

½ tsp Dijon mustard

Approx 1¼ cups (300 ml) lightly flavored oil (I use vegetable oil)

1 lemon

¼ small iceberg lettuce, separated into leaves, washed well, and dried

A few chives

Salt and freshly ground black pepper

To make the mayonnaise

1 Put the egg yolks in a clean bowl and whisk them together with the mustard—this is much easier if you have an electric whisk but if not, you'll just have to whisk by hand.

2 Next whisk in the oil, adding a few drops at a time and making sure each bit of oil is fully incorporated before adding the next.

3 As you whisk in more oil and the mayo starts to thicken, you can start adding the oil in very slightly larger quantities until you are steadily adding it in a thin stream.

4 Add a couple of tablespoons of bisque and the juice of half the lemon.

5 Whisk again and season with salt and pepper. You might want to thicken it slightly if it's too thin at this point. If the mayo splits, then it is possible to save it—just get a clean bowl and add a fresh egg yolk to it, then whisk the split mixture into it in the same way that you added the oil.

To serve

1 Now combine the lobster meat with a tablespoon or so of the mayo and mix. You may want a little more mayo, but don't go overboard—you really don't want to overwhelm the lobster flavor. Save the rest of the mayo for something else (it will be amazing in a shrimp mayo sandwich, or with a piece of fried fish).

2 Tear a few lettuce leaves into large pieces and scatter between two plates. Divide the lobster mayo mixture and arrange on top of the lettuce. Use scissors to snip the chives evenly over each pile of lobster meat. Cut the remaining lemon half into two wedges and serve with the lobster cocktail. Just make sure you tell your date all about the cooking process.

Song suggestion: *Rock Lobster* by The B52s.

Duck à la Pamplemousse

Weird, isn't it, how the classic and now terribly dated dish of duck à l'orange has a half-English, half-French name? Like we couldn't cope with saying "canard à l'orange" but wanted to sound a little sophisticated so turned our noses up at "duck with orange." Instead we ended up with something truly ridiculous. Duck, however, is a truly decadent ingredient if it is cooked well, and it's so damn good with citrus. Enter the most ridiculously named French fruit of all—the grapefruit. The pamplemousse. The bitterness of the grapefruit actually works really well here, and is a much better fit than the often-too-sweet oranges used in the original recipe.

Ingredients

1 grapefruit, halved

½ tsp honey

Pinch of sugar

2 duck breasts, weighing approximately 6 oz (170 g) each

1 tbsp butter

Salt and freshly ground black pepper

Serves 2

1 Preheat the oven to 340°F/170°C/Gas 3.

2 Squeeze the juice from one grapefruit half and mix with the honey and sugar. Peel the other half, using a sharp knife to remove all the white pith, and then remove peeled segments, again with a sharp knife. Finely chop the segments and add them to the juice, honey, and sugar mixture.

3 Pat the skin of the duck breasts dry with a piece of paper towel. Score the skin of each breast in a criss-cross pattern, taking care not to cut into the meat. Season well with salt and pepper and then place the breasts, skin side down, in a cold skillet or ovenproof pan.

4 Place the pan over a medium heat and fry the duck breasts for 7 minutes. Turn them over and add the honey and grapefruit juice mixture followed by the butter—take care as this will splutter in the pan.

5 Allow the butter to melt, basting the duck with the juices as you do so and tilting the pan to scoop up the juices.

6 Place the skillet or pan in the preheated oven and cook as follows: 5–6 minutes for pink; 10–12 minutes for well done.

7 Serve simply with some spinach or similar greens and perhaps a potato or five, if you're in the mood.

Profiteroles with Chocolate and Cherries

I swear I am on the verge of doing a little drool just thinking about profiteroles. I wanted to do something that wasn't stupidly hard like the spectacular croquembouche (a tower—and I really mean a tower) of profiteroles covered with glistening strands of spun sugar. I mean, you can make one of those if you like, don't let me stop you; it's just that this is a whole lot simpler. Don't be tempted to use milk chocolate for the sauce—it will be too sweet with the cream-filled profiteroles.

Ingredients

3 oz (80 g) butter

3 tsp superfine (caster) sugar

4 eggs

1 cup (125 g) all-purpose (plain) flour

Makes a stack of profiteroles that could, in theory, serve 2, 4, or even 6 people

To make the profiteroles

1 Preheat the oven to 425°F/220°C/Gas 7. Next, start on the profiteroles. Put the butter, sugar, and ¾ cup (200 ml) water in a pan and place over a low heat until the butter and sugar have melted. Once this happens, bring to the boil, then remove the pan from the heat and add the flour. Beat furiously with a wooden spoon until the mixture comes away from the pan. Leave the mixture to cool for 5 minutes, then beat in the eggs, one at a time. The result should be a mixture that is stiff and glossy. If you have an electric whisk, this is the time to use it.

2 Prepare two baking sheets by rinsing them with cold water and then just shaking off the excess rather than drying them completely. Using two teaspoons, spoon blobs of the mixture onto the baking sheets, making sure you space them well apart. Cook in the preheated oven for 18 minutes, or until well risen and golden brown. Remove from the oven and immediately make a small incision in the bottom of each one—this stops them collapsing in on themselves as they cool. Move to a wire rack to cool completely.

To make the vanilla cream

Ingredients

½ cup (150 ml) whipping cream

2 tbsp superfine (caster) sugar

1 vanilla pod

1 | The French call it crème Chantilly, so call it that if you want to sound fancy. Put the whipping cream and sugar in a bowl.

2 | Slit the vanilla pod lengthwise and scrape out the seeds using a knife; add the seeds to the bowl and whip until the cream just holds its shape.

To make the chocolate sauce

Ingredients

5 oz (150 g) bittersweet (plain) chocolate

3 tbsp whipping cream

Small knob of butter

Pinch of salt

8 cherries, to decorate

1 | Break the chocolate into pieces and put in a small pan along with the cream. Place over a low heat until the chocolate has melted and is combined with the cream.

2 | Stir in the butter and salt. Ideally, you want to serve this warm as it's a nice contrast to the cold cream in the profiteroles, so just keep it warm until needed.

To fill the profiteroles

1 | You can either be a fancy pants and try piping the cream in with a piping bag, or you can split the profiteroles in half and sandwich them together with the cream; it's up to you.

2 | Arrange them in a pile on a plate, in a sort of pyramid shape. When you're ready to serve, dribble the hot chocolate sauce over the top and dot with the cherries.

A Little Tipple

When choosing a drink, it really had to be something fizzy for this chapter—classy, elegant, and timeless. Well, provided you do use champagne and not Martini Asti, anyway. Thinking about champagne, I've just had a really cheeky idea. It's something I've seen people do IN REAL LIFE so I know it's possible, and it's called sabrage. Sabrage, if you're not familiar, is the act of opening a bottle of champagne with the back of a heavy knife or, traditionally, a saber. It's dramatic and really show-offy, but also really impressive. It basically involves exploiting the weak point on the neck of the bottle. If you are crazy enough to actually give this a go *checks legal cover* then here's what you will need to do.

1 Reconsider doing this.

2 MAKE SURE YOUR DATE IS STANDING BEHIND THE BOTTLE AND THE KNIFE.

3 Remove the foil and the wire basket from the top of the champagne bottle.

4 Identify the vertical glass line, that runs up the neck of the bottle.

5 Slide the back of the kitchen knife (not the blade) from bottom to top with as much force as you can muster (FFS don't let go of the knife at the end). It will hit the lip at the top of the bottle and you should keep following through with the swipe.

6 Neck and cork should be severed cleanly from the rest of the bottle.

7 Pour into glasses. DO NOT attempt to drink straight from the bottle, you will cut your lip. It's inevitable.

You can of course just be normal and open the champagne in the usual way. Don't let it pop out and fly off, by the way; that's just asking for trouble. Simply remove the foil and wire basket from the top, then take something like a dishcloth and use that to cover the top of the bottle and the cork while you gently ease it out. It will make a gentle, soft, ploop! noise and you will look like you've been opening champagne your entire life.

To Drink:

A Classic Champagne Cocktail

Once you've stemmed the blood flow following your failed flirtation with sabrage, you'll need a drink...

Ingredients

1 sugar cube

Dash of Angostura bitters

1 tbsp Cognac

Champagne

1 strip orange peel (remove any white pith)

Serves 1

1 Put the sugar cube into a champagne flute and add a dash of bitters on top of it. Add the cognac and then top up the glass with champagne.

2 Twist the orange peel over the top until you see a spray (see The Perfect Martini, page 23). Discard the peel and serve.

Song suggestion:
Mr Loverman
by Shabba Ranks.

CHAPTER nine

When Good Dates Go Bad

Cringe!

Ah, the dating horror story: so much fun to recall, just as long as you're doing the listening and not the telling. Of course, in preparation for writing this book I badgered all my mates for their dating histories, but funnily enough a lot of them weren't all that keen on having them published in a book. Weird. I promised anonymity! I begged! I made offers of drinks and meals and promised not to laugh TOO much, and still here I am with not a scrap of permission to publish stories about the worst dates of all time.

The Solution

Faced with no stories, I did what any reasonable person would do and asked Twitter instead. Here are some of the responses. I love how some of them start with, "so a friend… Yeah. Right." (I am **@FoodStories** in the following anecdotes.)

1 @FoodStories *"Weight Watchers date made me talk her through entire cooking process so that she could do her points correctly. No second date."*

Wow, she sounds like a barrel of laughs. Can you not have an evening off a diet for a date? Clearly not.

2 @FoodStories *"I tried to avoid looking incredibly guilty as a grateful date thanked me profusely for being so considerate and sourcing the vegan yogurt she'd just enjoyed. I hadn't."*

On a date, one should never be serving a yogurt as an individual course unless it is really, truly, the most shit-hot yogurt in the entire world. I say that as a huge fan of its tangy charms. Yogurt as an ingredient is one thing. A plastic pot of the stuff as dessert is another.

3 @FoodStories *"A friend made a 'low-key' pasta supper for newish beau. It had almonds in it. He hadn't mentioned his severe nut allergy. End = Epipen, plus ambulance."*

Oh dear. This cook could be accused of not paying enough attention to their date, for maybe not asking the right questions, for not being interested enough in their tastes and requirements. They could be accused of that, but in my view that would be completely and utterly WRONG. I'm sorry, but if you have a specific diet, allergy (particularly allergy!), or requirement of any kind, then it is your responsibility to tell your host. If you don't, then it's just really bad form, actually, not to mention really bloody unfair! Seriously, you could end up in hospital, you douche! Maybe it's worth checking? Hmm? Anyway, the fact remains that these things do happen, wires get crossed, and insecurities and anxieties stop information from coming out. The "friend's" date was apparently fine, by the way. The recipe that follows is for him.

Well, not actually FOR him, that would be bad, but it's in honor of the incident. It's great, provided you're not allergic to almonds.

Linguine with Pesto Trapanese

I've suggested 10 oz (300 g) of pasta for two people—I think this is a perfectly reasonable amount, but some actually maintain that 3 oz (75 g) is sufficient per person. This seems exceptionally stingy to me, unless you are serving other courses. I am rather greedy, though, so I'm going to leave it up to you.

Ingredients

10 oz (300 g) linguine

4 oz (125 g) blanched almonds

1 clove of garlic, peeled

Handful of basil leaves

4 ripe plum tomatoes, roughly chopped

3½ oz (100 g) pecorino cheese, grated

½ cup (100 ml) olive oil

Salt and freshly ground black pepper

Serves 2

1 Cook the pasta in plenty of boiling salted water according to the packet instructions.

2 Meanwhile, gently toast the almonds in a small frying pan, moving them around the pan so that they don't burn. They are ready when tinged golden in places. In a food processor, pulse the garlic, basil leaves, and a good pinch of salt. Add the almonds and pulse again. You want some texture to the pesto, so don't blend until completely smooth. Add the tomatoes, cheese, and oil. Pulse again and season with black pepper.

3 Once the pasta is cooked, spoon out a couple of tablespoons of the cooking water into a small bowl. Drain the pasta and stir a few tablespoons of the pesto through it (or more or less to taste). If the pasta looks like it needs loosening at this stage, add a little of the pasta water and mix through. Serve immediately.

4 @FoodStories *"A friend planned an elaborate dinner party to impress a girl at university and invited her and her housemates to feast. Think starter was goats' cheese (it was the nineties), roast chicken, pork stuffing, trimmings, homemade ice cream. Expensive stuff for a student. And wine too! He was crushed to see she wasn't tucking in—cooking was his trump card. Discovered she was vegan as he passed her the ice cream."*

See, again. **AGAIN**. OK, so you can imagine, can't you, they're young, they're not very confident, she decides not to raise the vegan thing. Maybe she's so nervous she can't speak or something? Seriously though, would it honestly be more awkward to say you're vegan, or to sit for an entire meal not eating anything, knowing that your date will be watching to see if you like it? Really? You're going for the former? And what about the housemates, why didn't they speak up? Had she asked them not to? In which case, bad. Had they decided not to off their own backs? Also bad.

5 @FoodStories *"He made a chili so spicy it actually burnt my tongue."*

Quite the achievement! Shows a remarkable confidence in your date's tolerance, don't you think? Either that or complete and utter obliviousness to one's own chili tolerance. Or perhaps he just didn't care. Anyway, overleaf I give you a recipe for a really good chili. I leave it up to you to decide just how much heat to pack into it.

Fiery, Smoky Chili

This is a one pan job, which means you can leave it bubbling away while you talk to your date and the air fills with the complex aromas of the three types of smoky chilli you so carefully sourced.

Ingredients

1 whole bulb of garlic

2 extra-large scotch bonnet chilies (optional, depending on how much heat you want)

olive oil, for drizzling

1 dried ancho chili

1 dried chipotle chili

1 tbsp cumin seeds

1 tbsp coriander seeds

4 tbsp groundnut (peanut) or vegetable oil, for frying

2½ lb (1.2 kg) stewing beef, cut into bite-size chunks

2 onions, diced

2 Romero peppers, diced

1 tbsp dried oregano

Splash of red wine

½ cup (100 ml) beef stock

3 x 14-oz (400-g) cans cherry tomatoes in their juice

1 heaped tbsp tomato purée

1 cinnamon stick

1 bay leaf

1–2 tsp red wine vinegar

2 oz (50 g) dark chocolate (70% cocoa solids)

1 handful fresh cilantro (coriander) leaves

14 oz (400 g) kidney beans, soaked overnight and cooked according to packet instructions (or use canned if you prefer)

Serves 4

1 Preheat the oven to 400°F/200°C/Gas 6.

2 Remove the outer papery layers from the garlic bulb (leaving the cloves intact and the bulb together) and cut the top ¼ in (½ cm) off the bulb. Put the garlic and fresh chilies in a small roasting dish,

drizzle with oil, and cover with foil. Roast for about 30 minutes until the garlic is soft. Remove from the oven and then tease the garlic cloves from their cases; set aside. Remove the seeds and skin from the chilies and set them aside.

3 Rehydrate the dried chilies by pouring boiling water over them and letting them soak for an hour or so. After this time, blend with a stick blender.

4 Toast the cumin and coriander seeds in a dry pan over a medium heat for a minute or so until they start to smell aromatic (keep giving the pan a shimmy so they don't burn). Transfer to a pestle and mortar or spice grinder and grind to a powder.

5 Heat a couple of tablespoons of oil in a large pan and brown the meat in small batches; set aside. Add a couple more tablespoons of oil to the pan and add the onions. Cook over a medium heat until soft and translucent and then add the diced peppers; cook for a few minutes. Add the roasted garlic and chilies, dried chili purée, ground spices, and oregano; stir for a couple of minutes and then add a good splash of red wine and allow to cook out for a few minutes.

6 Return the meat to the pan together with the beef stock, canned tomatoes, tomato purée, cinnamon stick, and bay leaf and simmer, covered, for at least 2 hours on a really low heat.

7 Stir in the vinegar, chocolate, fresh cilantro (coriander), and kidney beans 20 minutes before you want to serve. The chili is best eaten the day after you make it, with a touch more cilantro to finish.

6 @FoodStories *"My (then) boyfriend said he preferred his mum's Sunday roast."*

Mummy's boy. Shame she didn't teach him any manners, eh. Run a mile.

7 @FoodStories *"I once cooked dinner for a Michelin-starred chef. Substituting couscous for polenta was a low point. The polenta was to make potatoes extra crunchy. Didn't have any. Rather than use nothing I had a brain fart and decided to use couscous instead—small and grainy, how bad could it be? Really, really bad. Can you imagine? Potatoes coated in raw pasta."*

Sadly, I CAN imagine. Apparently he was the perfect gent about it and gave it the whole "it's just nice that someone cooked for me, usually people are too scared" spiel, which, in case you've never cooked for a chef, is what they always say when someone cooks for them. "You don't have to be nervous!" I remember one chef friend saying to me. I wasn't in the slightest, but hey, it's what they always say. I wouldn't want you to come a cropper with your roasties, however, so here's how to make a perfect batch. Yes, let's talk about food in batches, it's dead romantic.

Perfect roast potatoes don't need extras like polenta on the outside; what they need is to be parboiled for long enough, to be properly chuffed up around the edges, and to be thoroughly coated in hot fat. As long as those three parts of the method are correct, you should, no, you will end up with perfect roasties.

Perfect Roast Potatoes

Here is a recipe that should give you some really shit-hot roasties. Just don't substitute anything, yeah?

Ingredients

1 lb 2 oz (500 g) Maris Piper or Desiree potatoes

2 oz (50 g) goose fat or lard

1 sprig of rosemary

Sea salt flakes

1 Preheat the oven to 375°F/190°C/Gas 5. Put the fat in a small roasting tray and heat it in the oven while you prepare the potatoes.

2 Peel the potatoes and cut them into evenly sized pieces (not too small). Rinse them under cold running water for a few minutes to get rid of any excess starch. Place the potatoes in a large pan and fill with cold water. Season with salt and bring to the boil; cook for 10 minutes.

3 Drain the potatoes and leave them in the colander to steam dry for a few minutes. Don't skip this step. Give the colander a shake so that the edges of the potatoes get really roughed up—these will be your crispy bits.

4 Carefully remove the tray of fat from the oven and place the potatoes in it. Spoon the fat over the potatoes to make sure they are all completely covered. Roast in the oven for approximately 1 hour, or until golden brown all over. They won't need turning. Add the sprig of rosemary 10 minutes before the end of cooking. Once cooked, sprinkle the potatoes liberally with flaky sea salt.

8 @FoodStories *"Yeah… I got knocked out by a madwoman with a frozen chicken."*

This is obviously a clear favorite among the stories. Apparently the guy ended up in hospital with a nasty case of concussion. Of course I immediately asked how this happened, and he responded "She smacked me around the head with it," which I'd kind of guessed, but I laughed out loud anyway and then probed "dare I ask why?" He responded with "Funny thing is I have no memory of it due to the bump on the swede." OH HOW CONVENIENT. Of course this could be true. Brilliant dating story though, just brilliant. Not to mention a great advertisement for always buying fresh meat. Just when I thought I was done with hearing this story, he followed it up with "The hospital had a newsletter, and they sent me a copy, [it read] 'man admitted with frozen chicken injury.'" Amazing. Then, just to really round things off, "Ate the chicken on my own the next day… that showed it who is boss."

9 @FoodStories *"Once made ham omelet for what I thought was Thai ladyboy. Once in sack turned out to be retired Filipino wrestler."*

I'm fairly sure that last one was a joke, but you never know.

To Drink:

The Zombie

This is a drink that would have been extremely welcome in any number of the scenarios above. The Zombie is so named because of its effects on the drinker. It's strong, basically. Really strong. Be careful. DO NOT HAVE MORE THAN ONE. You can probably tell by this point that I like a drink, but hell, I'm not stupid. Apparently a man named Donn Beach invented the drink to help a hungover business client through an important meeting. I always think reeking of booze is the way to impress potential business partners, personally. Still, that is the story. Donn Beach, in case you're wondering, is the man credited with inventing tiki bars and restaurants, but we won't hold that against him.

Ingredients

1 measure dark rum

1 measure white rum

½ measure apricot brandy

2 measures pineapple juice

½ measure lime juice

½ measure orange juice

2 tsp confectioner's (icing) sugar

1 measure overproof rum

1 pineapple slice, to garnish

Serves 1

1 Shake everything apart from the overproof rum (and garnish) with ice in a cocktail shaker.

2 Pour into a glass and float the overproof rum on top. Garnish with the pineapple slice and serve.

Index

all-day breakfast in a can
  49–50
allergies 119
aphrodisiacs 92–3
  boozy Mexican hot
    chocolate 101
  figs 98–100
  sizzling fish 96–7
  steamed asparagus 94–5
asparagus 93
  steamed 94–5
avocado 92–3

batter, for Peckham Korean
  Fried Chicken 35
BBQ date 78–89
  bad juice 89
  "dirty" barbecue veg 86–7
  koftas 83–5
  redneck ice cream
    sandwiches 88
BBQs 78–80
  equipment 80–1
  lighting 81
Béarnaise sauce 20
bisque, for lobster 109
bread, cherry focaccia 71
breakfasts 14, 42–51
  disgusting 49–51
  eggs 43–7
burgers, "juicy lucy" 57–9

chicken, Peckham Korean
  Fried 33–8
chili 96, 121
  fiery smoky 122–3
Chimichurri sauce 21
chocolate 93
chocolate honeycomb
  mousse 63–4
chocolate sauce 113
cocktails 48, 65, 114–15
competitive cooking 29–31
Cook Off, the 28–31

dates 9–11
  disastrous 118–27
desserts
  chocolate honeycomb
    mousse 63–4
  ice creams 24–5
  Most Glorious
    Knickerbocker 26–7
  pomegranate and
    prosecco jelly 73
  redneck ice cream
    sandwiches 88
dinner date 14–39
  dessert 24–5, 26–7
  herb salad 22
  martini 23
  sauces 20, 21

steak 16, 18–19
"dirty" barbecue veg 86–7
drinks
  bad juice 89
  boozy Mexican hot
    chocolate 101
  champagne cocktail 114–
    15
  hot buttered rum
    cocktail 65
  martini 23
  Mustardy Mary (après-
    shag cocktail) 48
  Tinto de Verano 74–5
  Wrongungina 39
  the Zombie 127
drunk date 54–9
  "juicy lucy" burgers 57–9
  pimped instant noodles
    55–6
drunken cooking 32–8
duck à la pamplemousse
  110–11

eggs 43–7
  Donald's Perfect
    Scrambled 44
  eggy crumps 45
  Mumbai Disco Fry 46–7

figs 93, 98–9
  drunken baked 100
fish, sizzling with chili,
  ginger and scallion 96–7

ground rules 8–11

honeycomb 63–4
hot buttered rum cocktail
  65

ice cream 24–5, 88
insects 69–70

jelly, pomegranate and
  prosecco 72–3

Kajagoogoo sauce 36, 37
Kick-Ass koftas 83–4

linguine with pesto
  trapanese 120
lobster cocktail 107–10

marinades, for Peckham
  Korean Fried Chicken 34
martini, perfect 23
mayonnaise, for lobster
  109
movie date 62–5
  chocolate honeycomb
    mousse 63–4

hot buttered rum
  cocktail 65
Mustardy Mary (après-
  shag cocktail) 48

noodles, pimped instant
  55–6

oysters 93

Peckham Korean Fried
  Chicken 33–8
picnic date 68–75
  cherry focaccia with
    goats' cheese 71
potatoes, roast 125
profiteroles with chocolate
  and cherries 112–13

relaxed, staying 15–16
roast potatoes 125

salads, herb, with cherry
  tomato vinaigrette 22
sauces
  Béarnaise 20
  bisque (for lobster) 109
  Chimichurri 21
  chocolate 113
  Kajagoogoo 36, 37
  mint yogurt 84
  for Peckham Korean
    Fried Chicken 36–7
  smoky eggplant 84–5
scrambled lamb's brains
  51
special effort date 104–15
  champagne cocktail 114–
    15
  duck à la pamplemousse
    110–11
  lobster cocktail 107–10
  profiteroles 112–13
steak 16, 18–19

Twitter, @FoodStories 118–
  19, 121

vanilla cream 113
vegans 118–19, 121
vinaigrette, cherry tomato
  22

Wrongungina 39

yogurt 118–19
  mint 84

Zombie, the 127